INTERMODAL TRANSPORTATION

Quintessence, Legal Challenges & Impact on Current Transportation Insurance Schemes

JOSEPH TSHILOMB JK

authorHOUSE®

AuthorHouse™
1663 Liberty Drive
Bloomington, IN 47403
www.authorhouse.com
Phone: 1 (800) 839-8640

Published by AuthorHouse 10/10/2016

ISBN: 978-1-5246-4352-2 (sc)
ISBN: 978-1-5246-4351-5 (e)

Contents

Acknowledgement

The author is most grateful to:

* AuthorHouse, USA, for providing him with the opportunity to publish the second book under its famous roof and moral support while working on the book,

* To the MISSIONSSCHWESTERN von heiligen Namen Mariens, Our Lady Sisters in Osnabruck, Germany, for their legendary hospitality and

* The World Maritime University in Malmoe, Sweden, for the kind attention expressed at the author's first publication through the classification of the work in the Marine Insurance and Maritime Legislation category.

Eventually, it was not possible to name all the contributors to the project. Therefore, the author extends his sincere appreciation to all those who have not been mentioned!

Dedication

"Verba Volant, Scripta Manent."

Caius Titus

Preword

"Great dreams need more time and careful considerations for their successful achievement; therefore, it is advisable to proceed gradually until the desired building is raised and decorated."

These words were my advice to the author of the book in need of quality leisure time!

I was well aware that Mr Joseph Tshilomb was researching in the complex area of International Commercial Law and Global Trade.

He is a Swedish citizen and native from Elisabethville (L´Shi). I have known Mr Tshilomb during many years and have had many encounters with him talking about ethical issues associated with global and environmental aspects. He has shown a strong spirit of cooperation and motivation in order to achieve his project on Intermodal Transportation and Global International Trade.

I would like to emphasize the author´s kind and generous character. He is a cultivated gentleman and scholar. His mind is strong and stable; he argues in a tolerant and convincing way. He feels at home in international social surroundings.

He is able to change easily to different languages depending on the people participating in the conversation. One of the topics discussed with the author of this book was about the relative importance of freedom of contract in contractual relationships where one of the parties is in a disadvantaged position for economic reasons or weak health conditions.

With all these subjects in mind, I believe I have many good reasons to recommend the result of his research.

+ Erwin Bischofberger
PhD (University of Frankfurt)
Professor emeritus
Karolinska Institute
Stockholm, October 2011

Preface

The interface created by the conjunction of at least two modes of moving goods is a space which represents "Intermodal Transportation." This modern way of carrying goods in Unitized Units has got different denominations depending on geographic locations, the vehicles used for the carriage, the nature of the economic activities and other similar considerations.

Hence, different terms are used for the purpose of illustration of the interface created by the different modes of transport. They are: "Intermodal Transportation", "Multimodal Transport", "Combined Transport", "Multimodal Transport in Unimodal Transport" and "Roll-On & Roll-Off."

In this work the terms "Intermodal Transportation" have been preferred and include the other denominations above mentioned.

The Intermodal Transportation concept is mainly used in North America. It fits the modern conception of Carriage of Goods where the various segments of transportation create a unique transportation chain for more efficiency. This transportation chain consists at least of two of the following sections: sea transport, rail ways, truck services and inland waterways.

The denomination "Multimodal Transport" is the consecrated concept in Europe.

Other terms used for Intermodal Transport include the followings words: "Combined Transport" and "Through Transport".

"Combined Transport" is defined by the United Nations Economic Commission for Europe as the Intermodal Carriage where the major part of the European journey is by rail ways, inland waterways or sea and any initial and/0r final legs carried out by road are as short as possible.

The terms "Through Transport" are used for indication of unimodal successive carriers.

Eventually, it should be noted that it is possible to identify the Intermodal Transport in the various International Conventions associated with Carriage of Goods at the transhipments stage between various transportation segments.

Throughout this book practical illustrations would be done by means of relevant statistics, photography, historic account on different types of ships and location of the trade areas, such as port location, maritime routes as well as trade nature.

The presentation of this complex subject is made readable so that both specialists and

Academics and those in need of more knowledge could find practical interests in reading the book and reflecting on the main issues raised on the topic.

Methodology for the Purpose of a Thorough and Critical Understanding of Intermodalism in the International Carriage of Goods

No single academic can fully address all the main aspects of Intermodal Transport. Therefore, a multidisciplinary approach should be the appropriate method to the present study. As previously mentioned Intermodal Transportation includes engineering studies, economics, commercial operations, human resources development and requires a reliable and predictable legal regime.

Eventually, as far as the legal regime is concerned, the Classic Legal Method would not be appropriate to the genuine understanding of the subject: the International Intermodal Carriage of Goods is part of the needed commercial innovation in the course of Economic Globalization.

The author note with keen interest that strategic Logistics experts are still assessing the dramatic effects resulting from the bankruptcy of the South Korean container liner, **Hanjin Shipping**, at the time of completion of this book. Since, the Korean carrier was one of the major companies operating the containerized traffic, namely: the seventh firm in the world; the fact reveals the hidden vulnerability of the Transportation Industry.

Chapter I

Quintessence Of The International Intermodal Transportation Concept

Understanding the Intermodal Carriage of Goods is a requirement for people involved in International Trade. The whole philosophy behind Intermodal Transport is the packing of cargo into uniformly sized boxes (for example, containers) and then designing all carrying vehicles such as trucks, trains and ships for the swift, safe and efficient transport of these boxes, ideally using the "door to door" concept. All the parties involved in transactions agree on what the uniform size of intermodal carriage units should be.

In most countries the limiting width and length are governed by the road vehicles (8 feet 2.5 inches in UK). There is then the ISO (International Standards Organization) container of 8 x 8 x 20, 8 x 8x 30 and 8x 8 x40.

For the American trade with the availability of large road loads the 8 x 8 x 40 or FEUs (Forty Equivalent Units) are popular. On the other trades (Europe, Asia, etc...) the 8 x 8 x 20 is more common. (TEU or Twenty Equivalent Unit) is more common. An 8 x 8.5 x20 is now also popular.

The most used Intermodal Transport Unit is the Standard ISO (International Standards Organization) container. The ISO standards also apply to corner casting strength, floor strength, racking tests and the gross weight of the container.

Other Intermodal Transport Units include barges, car carrier, semi-trailers and rolling road (where lorries are carried on purpose-built low-floor wagon).

Thus, Intermodal Transportation is a larger concept that includes Containerization.

The introduction of Standard Containers for sea transport was an extension of a transport system that already existed within the United States. The move was initiated for some years ago by Trucking Companies and Railways that had adopted the Concept of a Single Unit which was detachable from its moving vehicle and could easily be transferred from one transport mode to another. The moving of the Carriage Unit with Connectivity Device from a transportation mode to another is the main character of any Intermodal (Multimodal) Carriage operations. Container tankers appeared at sea in the trade between New York and Houston in 1956. Afterwards, the California to Hawaï trade was containerized in 1958.

The first deep sea container service came in operations on the North Atlantic in early 1966 and was owned by Sea-Land, a company set up by Malcom MacLean, who was a trucker rather than a ship owner. Prior to that, he had experienced the merit of a cargo handling system that could use all three transport legs, namely: road, rail and sea. By this time, the major European liner shipping firms had also joined Containers Operations. The requirement for high-intensive investments inevitably led to consortia building-e.g. Overseas Containers Ltd (OCL) was a joint venture between P&O, Ocean, British and Commonwealth and Furness Withy. This trend will be the main features in Containerization.

Since the introduction of Containerization, shipping companies have widened their commercial interests to encompass the overall transport chain from the point of origin of the container through to the final destination.

Intermodal Freight Transport is essentially the concept of using more than one mode of carriage for moving goods from origin to destination. In the context of international transport the deployment of sea transport or air transport would be necessary and this mode of transport should be connected to another transportation leg to bring goods from or the airport/port. For example, iron ore from Latin America to the steel works in Germany would have to be moved by more than one mode.

In the case of Intermodal carriage an exchange of goods should be part of the overall chain of transportation. The transhipment could be done by transferring the goods from one mode to the other mode of carriage or by leaving the goods in the loading unit and transfer of the loading unit.

Gerhardt Muller (1995) defines intermodal transportation as 'the concept of transporting passengers and freight in such a way that all the segments of the carriage process, including information exchange, are efficiently connected and coordinated, offering flexibility.'

In particular for freight transport, the **United Nations Economic Commission for Europe defines Intermodal Transport as 'the movement of goods in one and the same loading unit or road vehicle, which uses successively two or more modes.'**

Hence, the following characteristics:

First of all, Intermodal Transport is not just a mode of Carriage of Goods like railways, barges or trucks are, but a concept for organizing the logistics chain. As bundling is an important element of creating efficient and effective transport chains, the character of Intermodal Transport enables this feature.

The most important elements of Intermodal Transport are:

* Two or more transport modes are used in a transport chain.

* The goods are carried in one loading unit which is standardized in order to be used on Several modes of transport.

* The exchange of the loading units between carriage segments makes transhipment in Terminals necessary.

The most important feature of the definition of Intermodal Transportation is the use of a **standardized loading unit**. Important for transport management is the possibility of bundling cargo (Packaging goods) to obtain efficiency in the Carriage of Goods. Bundling takes place on two levels. The first one is the bundling of loading units on a high capacity mode of transport: the manager would choose the ship, the barge, the cargo plane or the train.

The second level of bundling takes place by combining different shipments in one loading unit. Intermodal Transportation enables Logistics Managers to combine diverse shipments on most of the segments of the transport chain. Furthermore, efficiency is enhanced by using the standardized loading units moving through high quality transport infrastructure.

What are the containerized cargoes?1

Initially, the most appropriate cargo to be carried in containers consisted of general cargo, which means goods carried on board the ship in liner trade in packaged forms. However, with the extension of the service new types of containers were introduced to facilitate the carriage of non-standard cargoes. Special containers are limited in number in comparison with standard units, in spite of the fact that their use is increasingly growing. For heavy lift Open Top containers have been designed as reefer and ventilated containers are being used for frozen and chilled cargo and perishable agricultural products.

Containerization has been extended to bulk services. That is why it now dominates the deep sea liner maritime trade. Progress in containerization has led to intensive research into new packing, stowage and cargo handling methods in order to make the best use of Intermodal Transport units (containers, barges, etc...).

An enumeration of bulk cargoes which are now carried in containers is given below.[2]

*Wool

A large proportion of wool trade is currently carried in containers which consist of wool bales packed into TEU-containers giving an average weight of 18 tons.

*Motor cycles

---

[1] Alderton (P.M.), *Sea Transport: Operation and Economics,* Sunderland, Thomas Reed Publication Ltd, 1984, pp: 155-163; Stopford (Martin), *Maritime Economics,* London 1990, UNWIN HYMAN, p.p:194-196

[2] Stopford (Martin), *Maritime Economics,* London, UNWIN HYMAN, 1990, pp. 194-195

Motor cycle export trade from Japan is containerized. Up to 28 large motor cycles or up to 200 small ones can be carried in a FEU-container.

★Cotton

A total of 82 standard bales of cotton export from the US West Coast can be packed into a FEU-container.

★Wine

It is shipped by container either in cases or in 5,000-gallon bulk container tanks.

★Rubber

This product is usually shipped in bales. As appropriate response to the expansion of containerization, companies have now adopted standard bale size and packing of bales is done in shrink film instead of timber crates.

★Chocolates

British chocolates exports are containerized and shipped in insulated containers with special handling equipment designed to avoid condensation and tainting from previous carriages.

Chapter II

Legal Challenges In International Intermodal Transportation

1. Abstract

Multimodal transport is not a new concept. Nevertheless, it has initiated the process of integration of various age old transport modes, new technology in cargo unitization and electronic tracking systems. It has led to the facilitation of the carriage of goods in one seamless journey from the floor of the producer to the shelf of the store.

The overall transportation chain in international multimodal carriage of goods generally consists of the following legs: air carriage, carriage by sea, inland waterways, railways and truck services.[3]

Besides, the advent of container technology in transport of goods facilitated the introduction of consolidation or groupage services and contributed to the expansion of the international multimodal transport of goods. Consolidation or groupage means collecting. small parcels of cargo from several shippers (consignors) at the port of origin intended for several consignees at the point of destination.

Whereas the technical, commercial and economic aspects of multimodal transport have been adequately addressed in scholarly publications, the legal regime related to the liability of the multimodal carrier and its influences in the Insurance Industry are relatively new research areas with very limited available academic research.[4] The liability regime regulating the multimodal carriage of goods is unpredictable, unreliable and inadequate taking into account the overall expansion of the multimodal carriage of goods.

---

[3] McDOWELL (Carl E.), 'Shorter Articles and Comments: Containerization, Comments on Insurance and Liability'
HeinOnline-3 J. Mar. L. & Com. 500 1971–1972, 503–504

[4] Eun Sup Lee, 'The Changing Liability System of Sea Carriers and Maritime Insurance: Focusing on the Enforcement of the Hamburg Rules', HeinOnline- 15 Transnational Law. 241 2002, p.p.: 241–242; this need for new research was identified in the literature review done in the initial research proposal at The University of Edinburgh.

The legal unpredictability as referred to previously has a significant impact in the insurance cover available in multimodal transport.[5]

As a consequence of the described situation relating to the legal regime, the insurance industry has been coping with conflicting laws and regulation while settling claims arising from frequent and often capital intensive risks in multimodal transport of goods.[6]

Although many contractual solutions have been developed in the insurance industry in order to secure compensation and while standardized multimodal transport contracts are being used in order to solve legal issues and alleviate uncertainties, mandatory provisions related to the various transportation modes will still prevail if the scope of application for a specific convention of carriage is fulfilled.

For limitation purpose, the present research is restricted to cargo liability in Protection & Indemnity and Cargo Insurance; that is to say the liability of the carrier in International Multimodal Transport of goods for damage to goods, loss of goods or delay in delivery of goods. The three aspects of the liability pertaining to the Multimodal Carrier will be the main concern in this research. They are: the uniform liability (in the case the carrier liability is determined regardless of where damages have occurred), network liability (with varying limits depending on the applicable rules for underlying modes of transport) and the case where it is not known in what part of the transportation mode the damages have occurred.[7]

Within the framework of comparative law and private international law the rules related to the Multimodal Carrier liability are analysed using mainly the ideas and rules of the International Multimodal Transport based on the ICC/UNCTAD Rules, the regional rules developed (or being developed) by the European Union in the area of the International Multimodal Transport, including the Dutch, English and German legislations in Multimodal transport.[8] Mention should be made here that the ICC/UNCTAD Rules were conceived according to the UN Convention on Multimodal Transport (1980) which never entered into force. In addition, the European Single electronic Multimodal Document will be carefully analysed in this research study. The legal analysis disputes on the Multimodal Carriage contracts of goods are considered in their relationship with their insurance aspects (generally, the marine insurance).

---

[5] Hoeks (Marian), ***Multimodal Transport Law: The Law applicable to the multimodal contract for the carriage of goods,*** Kluwer Law International, The Netherlands, 2010, p. p. 35-37; McDOWELL (Carl E.), Op. Cit, pages 503-512; Chuah (Jason), ***Law of Internatioal Trade***, 3ʳᵈ Edition, THOMSON, p.p. 364-365

[6] McDOWELL (Carl E.), Op. Cit., p. 504-506

[7] Please, see for details Eftestol- Wilhelmsson (Ellen), 'The Rotterdam Rules in a European Multimodal Context', 2010, 16 JIML & C (10 pages)

[8] In this sense, see also, Hoeks (Marian), Op. Cit., p. 35.; Lamont- Black (Simone), 'Claiming Damages in Multimodal Transport: A Need for Harmonization' 2012, Tulane Maritime Law Journal, Vol. 36 (2), p.p. 707-724

The empirical method[9] with appropriate tools used in social sciences will improve the research with a comprehensive analysis of the Insurance market providing the needed cover (insurance policies in P&I and Cargo Insurance) for risks in international trade as seen in Private International Law.

Recent developments show marine insurance policies which integrate coverage for both traditional marine covers and landside exposures.[10]

Finally, in order to provide the overall picture which integrates the global international trade with its insurance implications cases such as MSC Napoli (Devon, 2008)[11], CARMACK Amendment (USA)[12] and Norfolk Southern Railways[13] v. James N. Kirby will be analysed.

2. RESEARCH BACKGROUND

It is the process of Unitization of Goods which culminated in the advent of Containerization which led to the present expansion of Multimodal Transport of Goods. Obviously, it consists of the high volume of commercial movements of boxes (containers) taking place internationally and on multimodal basis.[14]

Multimodal Transport was launched initially in Europe. However, the credit for the commercial and technical expansion is due to the United States. Thanks to the initial risky undertaking done by McLean (now Sea-Land) and Matson, the commercial basis of Multimodal transport of Goods was successfully established. And, already from the early stages great investments were required; that is to say high costs for initial testing risk in domestic and short-sea trades. Besides, a large fleet of sea-going vessels was needed, expensive cargo handling equipment, sophisticated port facilities and adequate container terminal were needed. The container transport development prompted special documentation requirements and many other container-related innovations.[15]

Briefly, Multimodal Transport led to the pressure for simplification and standardization in the following areas: advanced cargo-handling gear, increased size of trucks, larger bridges, through

---

[9] Robson (Colin) & Sheridan (J. C.), **Real World Research**, 3rd Edition, 2002, WITH SPSS, Vol. 18, pp.: 12-22; Gray (David E.), **Doing Research in the Real World**

[10] McDOWELL (CARL E.), Op. Cit., pp: 505-509

[11] Napoli MSC 2008 (Devon): this case established the right of the slot charterer to avail himself the limitation of liability recognized to the carrier (English Case law).

[12] The courts in the US have uniformly held that the Carmack Amendment pre-empts all state and common law claims and provides the sole and exclusive remedy to shippers for loss or damage in **interstate transit.**

[13] This is a consecration of an ocean carrier' s limitation of liability to the inland carriage of goods under a through ocean bill of lading (USA).

[14] McDOWELL (CARL E.), Op. Cit., pp: 503-505; Lamont-Black (Simone), Op. Cit., p.p. 707-724; IGP&I (Read the International Group of P&I Clubs), 'Chairman' s statement' ANNUAL REVIEW 2011/2012, page 5

[15] McDOWELL (CARL E.). Op. Cit., p.p. 504-505

—rate structures, new documents, customs procedures, and, last and particularly many legal aspects of commerce which are the object of this thesis.

Nevertheless, more important for lawyers, companies engaged in International Trade, the Transportation Industry and the Insurance Industry is the broad variation in regimes and limits of liability which apply to international commerce.[16]

Resulting from different legal regimes concerned with each mode of transport, the law of carriage of goods has evolved historically and functionally through separate transportation modes.[17]

As a result of the preceding statements, the Insurance Industry has been just coping with conflicting laws and regulations while settling claims for damages, loss of goods or compensation for delays in delivery of goods.

That is why the liability regime in Multimodal Carriage of Goods seems unpredictable, inadequate and unreliable.

3. CONTEXT AND AIM OF THE RESEARCH

Context of the research

The present research study is about the main legal issues in the liability of the multimodal carrier and the insurance risks in multimodal carriage of goods as seen from the claims handling perspective with regard to Protection & Indemnity Insurance, including Cargo Insurance aspects. It is placed in the area of European Multimodal Carriage of Goods (Transport Law), International Private Law and the International Trade Law.[18]

Taking a quick look at the law of **International Carriage of Goods**, the following observation needs to be mentioned for a better understanding of the research: the basic rule in Carriage of Goods is established in Article 3 in Hague Visby Rules which introduces the principle of the liability of the maritime carrier. The carrier has a duty of taking care of the goods during the carriage period.

Article 3, paragraph 2, of Hague/Hague-Visby Rules stipulates:

"Subject to the provisions of Article 4 …, the carrier shall properly and carefully load, handle, stow, carry, keep care for and discharge the good carried."

---

[16] Hoeks (Marian), Op. Cit., p. 36

[17] Hoeks (Marian), Op. Cit., p.p.: 41-43; De Wit (Ralph), **Multimodal Transport: Carrier Liability and Documentation**, Lloyd' s of London, 1995, p. 27-219

[18] Tetley (William), **Marine Cargo Claims**, Fourth Edition, Thomson ★ Carswell, 2008, pages 5-21; Chuah (Jason), **Law of International Trade**, Third Edition, Thomson ★Sweet & Maxwell, p. 1

This formulation was adapted at different periods of time and modes of transportation in order to meet the ever changing conditions in carriage of goods from bulk shipping to cellular container ships through the general cargo shipments context.[19]

It is argued that the main international effort in the work of harmonization of rules in carriage of goods was just the Hague/Hague-Visby Rules. In case of failure for the carrier to fulfil his main duty of taking care of the cargo, he will be held liable for compensation of damage.

Recent development in carriage of goods is characterized by the adoption of the United Nations Convention on Contracts for the International Carriage of Goods Wholly or partly by Sea, known as the **Rotterdam Rules**. There is uncertainty about the entry into force of the convention. The newly adopted Convention on Contracts for the International Carriage of Goods Wholly or Partly by Sea which is also called "Maritime Plus" instrument is intended to replace the three existing conventions relating to the ship owner liability.

In spite of the desirability of the rules established in the new convention, there is no unanimity as to the future effectiveness of the rules.

The representatives of P&I Clubs believe that the rules will add some extra costs in marine insurance.[20]

However, clubs are in favour of the idea of a single liability regime which would speed claims payments and reduce claims costs in the long term: a single standard would reduce uncertainty and enable claims to be settled faster. The rules are largely debated by practitioners, legal experts and scholars with deep insight in issues relating to the harmonization of the rules of carriage of goods and marine insurance.[21]

The convention contains a number of new and effective features. The scope of application of the convention would extend to door-to-door carriage and many of the beneficial aspects of existing conventions and regimes are retained.

In particular, it retains the existing concept of network liability, whereby liability and the applicable limits of liability for loss or damage to the goods occurring before or after the sea-leg would be a matter of any unimodal international instrument compulsorily applicable to the relevant mode of transport where the loss or damage occurs. The Convention retains the concept of fault-based liability found in The Hague/Hague-Visby Rules, but the standards and burdens

---

[19] Article 1, Montreal Convention
Article 17.1 for strict liability, CMR (Road)
COTIF-CIM (Railways), 1999, 23.1

[20] West of England REVIEW, 'Rotterdam Rules', West Of England Luxembourg, p. 1, 2012; See also the initial position of the International Group of P&I Clubs during the negotiations of the Convention

[21] D. Rhidian (Thomas), 'And then there were the Rotterdam Rules', (2008) 14 JIML, at pp. 189-190; Eftestol-Whilelmsson (Ellen), 'The Rotterdam Rules in a European Context', (2010), 16 JIML

of proof overall are more onerous for the carrier. It has provisions for electronic commerce and allows more freedom of contract in the liner trade by introducing the concept of **"Volume Contract"**[22] in carriage of goods.

The Rotterdam Rules address the issues related to jurisdiction and arbitration. Under the Rules cargo owners can effectively choose from a number of jurisdictions of the court where they can sue the carrier. As to the exclusive jurisdiction agreements contained often in contracts of carriage, they do not have primacy.[23]

The ability for cargo owners to choose from a number of jurisdictions may lead to a greater uncertainty for carriers and insurers and high legal costs due to the fact that courts of countries unfamiliar with such issues are asked to decide test cases arising under the Convention.

Placing the Rotterdam Rules in a European Multimodal context, Doctor Wilhelmsson concludes that the modified network liability system of the Convention represents a step forwards in the international regulation of the multimodal carrier liability. Currently, the European Union Consider the Rotterdam Rules as an alternative to the required international regime of the rules of Multimodal Transport.[24]

Aim of the research

It is assumed that the International Multimodal Transport should be regulated under **a unique liability regime** instead of separate liability systems, each for its mode of transport, as it is the case at the moment.[25]

The aim of this research is to find an adequate solution to the issue of the broad variation in regimes and limits of liability in Multimodal Carriage of Goods and to provide appropriate solutions to the highly frequent and capital-intensive risks of insurance covered presently in available insurance policies related to the International Multimodal Transport.

These solutions will be the contribution of the research to the process of harmonization of rules for the purpose of promotion of the Multimodal Carriage of Goods leading to the improvement in the global international trade.

---

[22] Non-mandatory regime for slot chartering and NVOCC

[23] West of England P&I Club, 'The Rotterdam Rules as seen by the P&I Club West of England', Review, 2012

[24] Eftestol-Whilelmsson (E), Op. Cit., (As amended, Swansea, September 6th and 7th 2012)

[25] Hoeks (Marian), Op. Cit., pages 43–45; De Wit (Ralph), Op. Cit., p. 3

4. RESEARCH FOCUS

The focus of the research is placed on the main legal issues related to the liability of the multimodal carrier and their impact on the insurance covering the specific risks in multimodal carriage of goods under the perspective of the protection and Indemnity Insurance. Cargo Insurance aspects in relation with carriage of goods will also be considered in the research.

5. LEGAL RESEARCH QUESTIONS

The first research question

In the context of multimodal transport where different transportation modes are regulated by differing legal regimes in addition to the uncertainty with regard to unlocalized damages/loss or delay in delivery of cargo, how will claims related to damages be assessed?

Subsidiary question

What happens in case of a damage which occurred in road or railways transportation leg when the main carriage had been performed onboard a sea-going vessel?

The second research question

What is the impact of the legal uncertainty and unreliability of the rules of multimodal transport in carriage of goods as defined in the first research question on the insurance covering the multimodal carrier liability (or Multimodal Operator) and the consignment?

The third research question

Is there any need for harmonization of the rules regulating the liability of the Multimodal Transport carrier and the regime of insurance covering the risks in multimodal carriage of goods?

Subsidiary question

What about the required insurance schemes in international multimodal transport of goods?

6. LEGAL RESEARCH METHODS

This section is dedicated to research methods[26] which will be applied to the research. The two main questions here are the following:

---

[26] For details on the appropriate methods, see McDOWELL (Carl E.), Op. Cit., p.p.: 504 – 512; Lamont-Black (Simone), Op. Cit., p.p. 707-724

What are the research methods to be applied to this study?

What is the relationship between the research questions and the methods, including the expected results of the thesis in using these research methods?

Legal Research Methods: Legal Methods and Empirical Method

Legal Methods

Two legal methods have been selected in this research: the method of solving the conflicts in Private International Law and the Comparative Law approach.

Method of solving the conflicts in Private International Law

As mentioned in the initial research proposal Doctor Marian Hoeks, Professor William Tetley and other writers successfully used the method of solving the conflicts in Private International Law in their legal analysis of the main issues in Multimodal Transport.[27]

This approach was also used in studies related to the insurance aspects in seaborne trade.[28]

The Private International Law can be defined as follows:

"A legal framework consisting of conventions, protocols, model laws, legal guides, uniform

documents, case Law, practice and customs as well as other documents and instrument

which regulate relationship between individuals in an international context."

The Private International Law deals exclusively with the legal relations of persons belonging to different States in which States as such are not parties.[29]

The rules of Private International Law are used as a procedure in order to determine which legal system and which jurisdiction' s rules apply to a given dispute. They apply when a legal dispute has a "foreign" element such as a contract agreed by parties located in different countries. The three main branches of conflicts of law in Private International Law are:

* The choice of law: the law to be applied to the conflict,

* The conflict of jurisdiction: deciding whether or not the forum court has the power by virtue of law to decide on the legal issue and

---

[27] Hoeks (Marian), Op. Cit., p.p 36–37 ; Tetley (William), Op. Cit., p.1, De Wit (Ralph), Op. Cit., p. 3

[28] Chuah (Jason), *Law of International Trade*, Third Edition, Thomson *Sweet & Maxwell, p. 1

[29] Home page www.oas.org/dil/private_international_law.htm on the 24th of September 2012

★ Enforcement of foreign judgments: deciding whether or not the forum court has the ability to recognize and enforce a judgment from an external forum within the jurisdiction of the adjudicating forum.

One of the main advantages of using the method of solving legal conflicts in Private International Law is that it leads to the harmonization of rules of law which is one of the objectives of this thesis.

Comparative Law Method

It is generally assumed that comparison is a technique, a discipline, an implementation and a method by which the values of human life, social relations and scientific activities are known and evaluated. The importance of this technique has been also recognized in legal research: there is a comparative method in law. Its essence lies in its attribute defined as a particular method of study, not the law of a specific country, but the general notion of law itself.[30]

This approach has given birth to a relatively new branch of legal study which is called "Comparative Law" whose aim is to study the laws of different countries in a comparative manner. The Comparative Law method, being basically a method of study, is considered as a process of studying foreign laws in comparison with local laws. Its function is to ascertain the differences and similarities in the legal rules, principles and institutions of two or more countries with a view to provide solutions for local problems (or for a harmonized legal regime in Private International Law). It is a needed discipline for maintaining order in the community through the knowledge and experience with others living in a foreign country.

Many attempts to define "Comparative Law" have been made by lawyers: some considering the comparative law approach as a specific branch of law whereas others define this approach as a tool for legal analysis.

In this thesis, the Comparative Law Method is mainly used as a tool for legal analysis in order to achieve harmonization in the current context of globalization in international trade law.[31]

Before showing the practical importance of the method of solving legal conflicts in Private International Law and the Comparative Law approach, the following concepts need to be clarified. They are: Comparative Law, Conflict of Law and Unification or Harmonization of law.[32]

In the strict sense, Comparative Law can be defined as the theoretical study of legal systems by comparison with each other. Its tradition goes back over a century.

---

[30] For further details, see Monrirov (A) & Naude Fourie (Andria), **_Vertical Comparative Law methods: Tools for Conceptualising the International Rule of Law_**

[31] Norman (Paul), 'Comparative Law', published at www.nyulawglobal.org, on the 27th of September 2012 and updated in August 2007

[32] Norman (Paul), Op. Cit., www.nyulawglobal.org as updated in August 2007

In recent years, it has gained in practical importance for the reasons presented below.

The first one is the increased globalization of world trade that involves the need to perform commercial transactions in unfamiliar (foreign) legal systems.

The second reason is the move towards harmonization of laws, and more recently towards codification within the European Union where several legal traditions coexist.

It should be mentioned that there are publications and internet resources that collect legal materials from several jurisdictions without performing a strict comparisons of these resources which can be used as real tools to be developed through the proper Comparative Law approach. These legal materials can be considered as a loose form of Comparative Law.

Concluding the section dealing with the legal methods, a clarification of concepts needs to be done as to the use of the following terms: Comparative Law, Conflict of Laws and Unification or Harmonization of Laws.

These three topics are distinct, but closely related.[33]

Briefly, it can be mentioned that **conflicts of law, or (usually) private international law**, concerns national or domestic legal rules applicable in situations involving the law of another jurisdiction. This may be another country, or in the case of federations, another state.

As to the terms **"Unification of Law or Harmonization of Law"**, the following explanation can be given. It is a process that grew out of the need to simplify conflict of law rules, often by international conventions. The unification of law has acted on both the national and international levels.[34]

Currently, there are two main sources of International Uniform Law: the Hague Conference on Private International Law and UNIDROIT[35].

The **Comparative law method** has been generally defined as a theoretical study of various legal systems by comparison with each other in order to improve the national legislation (cope with the increased globalization of the international trade).[36]

Empirical Method of the Research

The empirical approach suggests that some phenomenon is studied through observations.

---

[33] For details, see Duncan (Alfords), ***Guide on the Harmonization of International Commercial Law***

[34] Norman (Paul), Op. Cit. (as updated)

[35] UNIDROIT stands for The International Institute for the Unification of Private Law, in Rom, Italy

[36] Norman (Paul), Op. Cit. (as updated)

In order to achieve a successful empirical research, the information collected for that purpose should be presented in a systematic way, submitted to a critical analysis and presented to the wider community with caution.[37]

In the context of this research, the empirical study will be conducted according to the research tools generally admitted in social sciences, such as surveys in the Insurance industry and in-depth interviews with a relevant focus group. Assumption is made that the tools to be used in the empirical method will provide a better understanding of what is actually happening in the insurance industry which is just coping in order to cover the new risks in multimodal transport.[38]

The empirical approach will mainly be qualitative and inductive in this research.

Both data collection and data analysis will be performed with clarity so as to be as explicit as possible about the outcome of the research.

At present, the identification of the main actors in the insurance market has been done.

The design of the survey to be carried in the research and the questionnaire to be submitted to the focus group will be conceived in accordance with the main challenges facing the insurance industry and International Trade.

Relationship between the research questions and their methods, including the expected results in using these research methods in the thesis

The first research question

The first research question is obviously linked to the legal methods: the main legal issues pertaining to the liability of the multimodal carrier are a clear illustration of conflicts to be solved according to the rules elaborated in Private International Law.

Taking the example of limitation of liability in a claim for damages to a container occurred in another country, the court of the forum would firstly have to decide whether it has jurisdiction on the case or not. Once the question on jurisdiction has been solved, the judge who has to decide on the claim should decide according to the rule of law applicable to the claim. Both the jurisdiction on the case and the law to be applied to the conflict will be determined according to the method of solving the conflict in Private International Law.

---

[37] Darlington (Yvonne) & Scott (Dorothy), **Qualitative Research**, Australia & Philadelphia, 2002, p.p.: 66-77; Robson (Coun), **Real World Research: Approaches to social research**, 3rd Edition with SPSS, Vol. 18 (This book provide a clear route of the various steps in the empirical research); Gray (E. David), **Doing Research In The Real World** ("Research in this context is a systematic and organized effort to investigate a specific problem that needs a solution)

[38] Reliability in performing the empirical study and validity of its result are the key words in the empirical method.

In addition to the Private International Law approach, the method used in Comparative Law will be used to find a solution to the first research question: this is the actual legal practice which is the combination of the two mentioned methods for the legal issues with regard to the liability in multimodal carriage of goods.[39]

Asking the first research question and using both the method of solving the conflict in Private International Law and the Comparative Law approach will lead to the identification of the main legal issues, the definition of the scope of the study and the aim of the research study. Needless to mention that the solutions to the legal issues in Private International Law normally lead to the process of Unification or Harmonization of rules.[40]

For this purpose, the method of solving the conflicts in Private International Law should be completed by the method of Comparative Law which allows finding in the law of other countries the needed solutions to the legal issues.

The second research question

The second research question examines the impact of the main legal issues on the Insurance Industry. Here, again, the appropriate methods are the legal ones, namely: solving legal conflicts in Private International Law and the Comparative Law Approach.

Once this impact is defined, the solutions provided by the Insurance Industry will be presented. This approach is preferred in the traditional method for analysing admiralty jurisdiction over contract disputes and its application to marine insurance (That is to say from carrier liability issues to insurance issues).

This research does not intend to investigate in details the question of liability of the carrier: This is to be assumed in the context of the thesis. The aim is rather to focus on the less contentious areas of more procedural nature, such as issues of quantification of damages, type of damages, notification of damages, time bars and extinction of action, limitation of amount of carrier liability and so on.

It is argued in support of this position that the invention of marine insurance was the result of the need on the part of ship owners and merchants to make good loss arising from the destruction of property by tempest or other peril of the Sea.[41]

---

[39] Hoeks (Marian), Op. Cit., p. 36; McDOWELL (Carl E), Op. Cit., pages 503–512

[40] Tetley (William), Op. Cit., p.1; Hoeks (Marian), Op. Cit., p. 36; De Wit, Op. Cit.:, P 1-219

[41] Derrington (Sarah), 'Marine Insurance Act 1906 – Introduction', Marine Insurance Act 1906 (Australia) at www.findlaw.com.au/articles/780/marine-Insurance-act-1906 --introduction.aspx, the 12th of April 2012

The third research question

The primary issue in this legal question is about achieving harmonization in the rules dealing with multimodal carriage of goods.

It is assumed that there is a broad variation in regimes and limits of liability which apply to the international regimes of carriage of goods and that the method of solving legal conflicts in Private International Law is the most appropriate for solving these legal issues.

In order to illustrate the sharp variations in exposure of the cargo owner who relies solely on carrier liability to protect his goods during a multimodal through shipment and to suggest the current legal problems which can arise, it is useful to refer to the major legal liability limits applicable to rail, highway, air transport and ocean carriage both in the national legislation and abroad. Hence, the importance of the method of Comparative Law in this context of a globalized international trade.

The combination of the methods of solving legal conflicts according to the rules of Private International Law and the approach of Comparative Law will lead the research to the needed Harmonization of the rules relating to the Multimodal Carrier Liability.

The need for such a harmonized regime will be analysed both from the perspective of the civil law legal system and the common law view point.

The subsidiary question to the third research question

It is assumed that the appropriate answer to the third research question will require the combination of the legal method and an empirical analysis.

For this purpose, the method of solving legal conflicts in Private International Law will be used in order to define the **critical path in litigation with regard to the specific risks in Multimodal Transport** which include damages occurring at goods in transit, unlocalized damages, damages occurring at container terminals, damages on goods occurring between ocean carriage and road/railways transportation legs.

These risks will be defined according to the legal approach of Private International Law.

Having defined the risks in Multimodal Transport, the research will analyse in depth these risks in the International Insurance Industry through the empirical method.

The final stage of the process will be the design of more suitable Insurance policies in response to the present global challenges in relation with the issue of Insurance Policies in Multimodal Transport of Goods.

The improved Liability Regime of the Multimodal Carrier and the development of efficient Insurance Policies covering the identified specific risks impeding currently the large scale expansion of the International Multimodal Carriage of Goods will offer financial and adequate legal protection to the multimodal carrier, provide more security to the cargo owner (shipper) and promote the Global International Trade.

Currently, Multimodal Transport studies are considered as an emerging area of strategic area. The following section will be about the main topics that need to be developed in further studies.

7. Topics for further studies on the Law of Intermodal Transport

★Theoretical perspectives

I Multimodal Transport of Goods: Legal Concept, History & Recent Development

The thesis will mainly be dedicated to the multimodal transport law within the European context.

II Multimodal Contract of Carriage of Goods

The idea of multimodal contract of carriage of goods as a "**sui generis**" is explored here. Another issue to be tackled is how to conciliate the concept of freedom of contract with mandatory rules in multimodal carriage of goods. An important question in this chapter will be about the concept of freedom of contract in common law and its large impact in International Trade Law.

III Rules of the of the International Multimodal Contract and Unimodal Transport

Regimes

The topic will be devoted to the definition of the multimodal contract and the identification of the rules dealing with multimodal arrangements in unimodal transport regimes. The provisions of the Rotterdam Rules in relation with multimodal carriage of goods will be of a particular interest in this study.

IV Main Legal Issues in Multimodal Carriage of Goods and their Impact in Insurance (P&I and Cargo Insurance)

The legal regime in international multimodal transport is unreliable, unpredictable and characterized by lack of uniformity. The difficulty for finding the relevant rules to apply in P&I Insurance is shown in this chapter. Different transportation mode regimes, the existence of three various maritime convention regimes along with difficulties inherent to damages that have occurred in third countries and the particular questions of conflict of laws in Private International Law as seen from the P&I Insurance (and Cargo Insurance) will constitute the subject of this chapter. Legal sources, case law legislations and other relevant cases of scholarly character will be used for illustration purposes.

V Making a Claim for Damages in Multimodal Carriage of Goods and the means of defence in favour of the carrier

Making a claim for damages is basically holding the carrier liable for damages in order to get compensation. The claim handling process will imply some of the main legal issues dealing with the carrier liability such as carriers' defences or exemptions of liability, limitations of liability, deciding on the relevant liability regime and jurisdiction, the rules regarding the claim delay and the interface between P&I Insurance and Cargo Insurance.

VI Insurance Claims Assessment

This proposal is intended to illustrate how claims are being managed by the Insurance Industry in the situation of lack of uniformity and predictability of the legal regime in multimodal carriage of goods. The three points which are going to be developed are the following:

* Settlement within the Insurance Industry (according to the contract of insurance),

* Jurisdiction assessment,

* Arbitration and

* Suggestions of improvement in litigation.

VII Recent development in insuring the risks in Multimodal Transport of Goods

The author argues for an extension of the P&I Marine Insurance related to the sea transport to the specific cover needed for insurance in multimodal carriage of goods.

VIII Harmonization of the Rules dealing with the Liability Regime in Multimodal Carriage of Goods and Improvements in Insurance Facilities with regard to New Challenges facing the Insurance available in Multimodal transport

The need for harmonization of the law of multimodal carriage of goods should be assessed through a comprehensive study and proposals for improvement in insurance facilities could be designed.

8. LITERATURE REVIEW

The purpose of this section is to illustrate the current state of the research in the law of Multimodal Carriage of Goods as seen from the Protection and Indemnity Insurance perspective in order to indicate the place of the thesis in scholarship. This comprehensive review is articulated around the following research statement.

The broad variation in legal regimes with various limitation rules of liability in Multimodal Carriage of Goods results in the unreliability, unpredictability and inadequacy of the present international regime in Multimodal Transport of Goods.

The commercial risks associated with the modern Multimodal Transport of Goods need to be addressed properly in order to prevent a general exoneration of the carrier through contractual arrangements, to protect the financial interests of the consignee (or shipper) and to ensure that the liability system in Multimodal Transport of Goods will contribute to the promotion of International Trade.

The Multimodal Contract of Carriage is "Sui generis" by nature.

This thesis is in favour of harmonization of the rules of the International Multimodal Carriage with regional legal systems and the consecration of the principle of freedom of contract.

Eventually, the appropriate and efficient research methods in the study of the liability in respect of the International Multimodal Transport are the method of solving the conflicts in Private International Law and the comparative law approach.

The above research statement is backed in the legal literature.

The multimodal carriage contract gives rise to much speculation, especially while considering the law applicable to the contract or to the claims resulting from it. It is argued that multimodal transport is very profitable in general, since it reduces transport costs and enhances efficiency, but the current legal framework does not complement the technical progress made in Carriage of Goods.[42] Modern day transport law has no adequate means to create certainty as to the legal consequences of any loss, damage or delay resulting from multimodal carriage when contracting parties are entering into a multimodal transport agreement. It does not even seem to offer enough clarity when loss has occurred. This is not a desirable situation for a branch of International Trade Law which should enhance and promote commerce under the basis of legal certainty. In addition to that, courts may have different interpretations of conventions, a situation leading to differing decisions.[43]

Such differences stimulate forum shopping, thus high costs of litigation. This problem has been addressed by means of an analysis of the current legal framework in relation to multimodal carriage and it has been shown that the applicable rules of Private International Law (in multimodal transport contract) and the options provided by the choice of law based on contractual conditions

---

[42] McDOWELL (CARL E.), Op. Cit., p.p. 503-505

[43] That is to say differing decisions at the national level (first level jurisdiction decisions versus appeal decisions) and at international level (with different decisions from courts belonging to different countries).

lead to the law applicable to a multimodal contract. This investigation was made through a comprehensive study of the legal systems of Germany, the Netherlands and England.[44]

Recently, a relevant research has been published on CMR carrier liability in the Netherlands and Germany and its influence in the development of the European Private Law.[45]

Recent Development on CMR Carrier Liability

The main concern is about the liability of CMR Carrier, namely about the interpretation in the European context of articles 29, 31 and 32 in the convention.[46]

There are different views in the interpretation of the aforementioned articles between Germany and the Netherlands. Besides leading to different outcomes concerning the exact liability of the CMR carrier, there is also the possibility that parallel legal actions are pursued on different sides of the border which may both bring about enforceable judgements. These are actions that are started between the same parties and on the same grounds. The most characteristic illustration of this undesirable situation is certainly the TNT v. AXA Case that has recently been judged by the European Court of Justice (ECJ).[47]

This judgement is used to illustrate the current legal situation. It can also assist in highlighting the advance of the European law.

The ECJ demonstrates in TNT v. AXA that even if priority is granted to such older international regimes, it can be withdrawn if the principles underlying the conflicting regulation are not observed. It is argued that the EU has exclusive competence to enter into an international agreement where the agreement affects EU rules according to the AETR doctrine.[48] In addition, certain areas of shared competence become exclusive EU competence as the EU adopts internal legislation and, thus excludes Member States' action externally.

According to article 17 (1) CMR, the carrier takes upon himself an 'obligation de resultat', since he promises to carry consignments from one place to another without changing the cargo in any way within the agreed timeframe. If the carrier fails to produce the agreed result, he is liable for any loss of goods that may have resulted or up to the amount of the carriage charges for any

---

[44] Hoeks (Marian), Op. Cit., p.p.: 35–37

[45] Hoeks (Marian), 'Liability, jurisdiction and enforcement issues in international road carriage CMR (Road) Carrier liability in the Netherlands and Germany and the influence of the EU', Eighth Annual International Colloquium on Carriage of Goods-Sea Transport AND Beyond, 6-7 September 2012, Swansea University, p.p. 1-13

[46] This is a further development in relation to Doctor Marian Hoeks's thesis as developed in "Hoeks (Marian), *Multimodal Transport Law: The law applicable to the multimodal contract for the carriage of goods, 2010*

[47] ECJ 4 May 2010, Case C- 533/08 (TNT Express Nederland BV v. AXA Vrsicherung AG)

[48] ECJ 31 March 1971, Case 22/70 Commission v. Council (1971) ECR 263

delay, besides having to make restitution for the carriage charges, custom duties and other charges incurred in respect of the carriage in proportion to the loss.[49]

There is only one escape from liability for the carrier and that is the force majeure defence and the force majeure related exonerations found in articles 17 (2) and 17 (4) CMR.[50]

Force majeure in article 17 (2), CMR

The force majeure provisions in the CMR have two important aspects: Material aspect and the procedural one. An important part of the procedural aspect is the distribution of the burden of proof which is laid down in article 18 CMR.[51]

In order to be exonerated, the carrier has to demonstrate that the loss, damage or delay was not caused by his wrongful act or neglect, but rather through circumstances which he could not avoid and the consequences of which he was unable to prevent, or due to the inherent vice of the goods. What can be deemed "circumstances which the carrier could not avoid and the consequences of which he was unable to prevent is determined in the Netherlands by the Oegema v. AMEV judgement of 1998 from the Dutch Supreme Court, the Hoge Raad, which was confirmed in Vos Logistics v. AIG in 2009.[52]

Nevertheless, it has been found that the BGH (German federal court) accepts the defence concerning an armed robbery of a moving truck as cases of force majeure whereas there is no example in Dutch cases where an armed robbery has been considered as case of force majeure.[53]

The loss of limitation of liability for CMR Carriers: wilful misconduct and its equivalent in article 29 CMR

Apparently, the criterion used in Germany is the same as that used in The Netherlands.

In the Netherlands, the default equivalent of wilful misconduct is called "conscious recklessness" which the Hoge Raad defined as reckless behaviour by a party who is aware that damage or loss is

---

[49] Article 23 CMR

[50] The terms "force majeure" is a French legal concept which is also commonly used in the Netherlands for the unavoidable circumstances defence in article 17 (2) of the CMR Convention. Although this terminology is not used in Germany there is only mention of the standard 'auberste' (Wirtschaflich, Zumutbare Sorgfalt. In the English legal sphere the expression "standard of utmost care is consecrated. The terminology "Force Majeure" is used in the following with the reservation that the force majeure referred to is a specifically CMR-tailored version; Hoeks (Marian), Op. Cit., Swansea Colloquium, August 2012

[51] Article 18 (1) CMR states that the burden of proving the loss, damage or delay due to one of the specified cases in article 17 (2) shall rest upon the carrier.

[52] HR 17 April 1998, NJ 1998, 602 (OEGEMA/AMEV); HR 24 April 2009, NJ 2009, 204 (Vos Logistics v. AIG

[53] Hoeks (Marian) Op. Cit., Swansea Colloquium, August 2012.; BGH, 13 November 1997, I ZR 157/95, TranspR. 1998, 250, VersR 1998, 872; BGH 28 February 1975 – I ZR 40/74, NJW 1975

likely to result from that behaviour. Nevertheless, this norm which is identical to similar German legal provisions on the surface is interpreted quite differently in the Netherlands.

In two judgements, both pronounced on the 5th of January 2001, the Hoge Raad determined that conscious recklessness exists when the acting party or the party failing to act is aware of the danger inherent to the act or failure to act and is also aware that the chance that the hazard will come to pass is larger than the chance that this will not happen, but acts or fails to act in spite of this.[54]

With this definition, the Hoge Raad established a very high bar which is almost unreachable.[55]

Briefly, there is a large discrepancy in the manner in which article 29 CMR is applied in the Netherlands and Germany. In Germany the standard applied may be somewhat stricter, but it is possible that a court deems the conditions met. On the other hand, the norm applied in the Netherlands can be assimilated to an insurmountable wall.

In conclusion, perhaps because this problem has swelled to unreasonable proportions, the discrepancies between the outcomes of procedures in Germany and the Netherlands have slightly been reduced in recent years.

The author has noticed further legal research studies initiated by Professor Hoeks on the issue. Relevant questions raised would be addressed in a future research.

---

[54] HR 5 January 2001, NJ 2001, 391

[55] Hoeks (Marian), Swansea Colloquium, August 2012 ; HR 5 January 2001, NJ 2001, 391 (Overbeek/Cigna); HR 5 January 2001, NJ 2001, 32 (Van der Graaf/Philip Morris I)

Two legal instruments have been used for that. In Germany the doctrine of "**Mitverschuden**"[56] was introduced to temper the liability of the carrier unable to invoke any of the CMR liability limitations.

In the Netherlands on the other hand the "**Verzwaare stelplicht**"[57] was created to achieve the opposite: the concept of aggravated assertion duty was used to open up the possibility to remove the liability limitation provision in case the carrier fails to provide sufficient information on the circumstances of the loss.[58]

Recent court decisions with regard to CMR litigation may have introduced the question concerning the relation between the international carriage conventions and EU law in international transport

---

[56] According to a ruling of the German Fiscal Court BFH, in application of the doctrine, depreciation is limited when the repair bill of a car is higher; Judgement of the BFH from the 24th of November 1994, IV R 25/94 BstBI II, 1995, 318 at www.rechtplus.de/witeile/db_witeile/u on The 9th of November 2012

[57] The concept is similar to situations in Common Law where the carrier has been reckless when the damage occurs; the French and the Belgian civil law apply the concept of "faute tres grave (inexcusable) du conducteur"

[58] Hoeks (Marian), Op. Cit., Swansea Colloquium, p.5

law. **Does the ECJ have the authority to restrict the application of the CMR? It is argued with relevance that this is the case in the TNT v. AXA proceeding.**[59]

Another issue in the legal literature is dealing with the Rotterdam Rules in a European Multimodal context. The modified network liability system of the Convention represent certainly a step forwards in the international regulation of the multimodal carrier liability.[60]

However, this is limited to Multimodal Contracts of Carriage with a sea leg. Currently, the position of the European Union is that the Rotterdam Rules are an alternative to the solution for finding the adequate regime in multimodal transport law.[61]

The liability of the multimodal carrier and documentation issues have also been covered with a comparative study of the law in Belgium, France, Germany, the Netherlands, the United Kingdom and the USA.[62]

Further, the general law of obligations (both contract and tort), which differs considerably between countries has been analysed, taking into account how it applies to a multimodal contract. A general description of the relevant concepts in the law of obligations of the countries mentioned above has been given, followed by an account of the attempts which have been made at harmonization of multimodal transport. Transport documents and the problems which they generate have been studied and supported by a score of practical examples on what can go wrong in a multimodal transport operation, where the legal dangers lie and how they can be avoided.

The complex and important problem of the liability of third parties, who have been employed as servants, agents or independent sub-contractors by the carrier, vis-à-vis the cargo interests is discussed.[63]

Besides Doctor Marian Hoeks and Doctor Ralph de Vit´s research, the treatise on multimodal transport rules written by Hugh M. Kindred and Marry R. Brooks[64] deserves mention in this research

---

[59] Hoeks (Marian), 'Liability, Jurisdiction and enforcement issues in international road carriage CMR carrier liability in the Netherlands and Germany and the influence of the EU', Eighth Annual International Colloquium on Carriage of Goods- Sea Transport And Beyond, 6-7 September 2012, Swansea University

[60] Eftestol-Wilhelmsson (Ellen), Op. Cit., p.p.: 1-10

[61] Eftestol-Wilhelmsson, 'Paper presentation…', Eight Annual International Colloquium on Carriage of Goods- Sea Transport And Beyond, 6-7 September 2012, Swansea University

[62] De Wit (Ralph), *Multimodal Transport: Carrier Liability and Documentation*, LLP, Lloyd's of London, London, 1995 ….

[63] De Wit, Op. Cit., p. 437

[64] Kindred (Hugh M.) & Brooks (Mary R.), *Multimodal Transport Rules,* Kluwer Law International, Dordrecht, The Netherlands, 1997

This book offers an insight into the complex legal regimes governing multimodal transport which is carefully considered in its commercial context and influences operating in the market. It is specified that there has been little documented experience with multimodal cargo casualties and even less litigation. Hence, the analysis of the multimodal rules is performed from first principles.

The authors discuss the common considerations of liability in the multimodal rules. The following issues are identified:

a)   What is the kind of cargo damage?

Cargo injury can be defined as loss of cargo, cargo damage or delay in good delivery.

b)   What is the basis of liability for loss, damage or delay?

The answer is that it depends on whether the cause of cargo injury can be localized or not.

c)   What is the extent of liability for loss, damage or delay?

It depends on:

- the value of the cargo damage,

- the applicable limit of liability,

- whether additional business losses were suffered and are compensable,

- whether an aggregate limit of liability applies and

- whether the limits of liability may be exceeded.

Legal issue about the container

The main legal issue about the container is about the amount of limitation of the carrier's liability.[65] Indeed, the container can be perceived as a package or as part of the ship with the implication on cargo worthiness or seaworthiness. This is an important issue in multimodal carriage of goods. It could be a good idea to look at the recent cases on the issue and see how the courts are deciding on the topic in various countries. Another question for further discussion on the topic of container would be the requirement of ship stability in connection with loading and lashing of containers which has now a significant impact on the insurance related to the goods carried in the container (P&I Insurance).[66]

---

[65] Stevens (Frank), 'Liability for defective containers: charting a course between seaworthiness, care for the cargo and shipper liabilities', The Eighth Annual International Colloquium on Carriage of Goods- Sea Transport and Beyond, 6-7 September 2012, Swansea University (Paper presentation)

[66] Here, the rules dealing with ship stability and safety at sea have a significant impact on insurance issues.

It has been found out that the examination of the variation in regimes and limits of liability which apply to international trade leads inevitably to the consideration of insurance issues with regard to the liability of the carrier for cargo claims and Cargo Insurance (in protection of the cargo owner or consignee).[67]

Available research studies on the relationship between multimodal carrier liability and insurance, especially the Protection & Indemnity Insurance, are neither systematic nor analytic.[68]

Therefore, a comprehensive study addressing specifically these insurance aspects in order to assure the expansion of the Multimodal Carriage of Goods and the promotion of International Trade is needed. This research study endeavours to analyse the question of the liability of the multimodal carrier with its impact on the insurance aspects in carriage of goods.

9. IMPORTANCE OF THE STUDY IN SCHOLARLY RESEARCH

The research fills a gap in the current scholarship: its aim is about finding more appropriate rules to the main issues identified in the area of carrier liability and insurance cover in International Multimodal Transport Law.

This thesis is unique in the sense that it represents a comprehensive study dealing exclusively with the issues of the International Multimodal Transport mainly from the Protection and Indemnity Insurance perspective.

This is a new research in the International Multimodal Transport Law. Its importance lies in the fact that the International Multimodal Carriage of goods has been witnessing a steady expansion with regard to the single transport mode: the use of Multimodal Carriage of Goods is being promoted namely in the European Union for economic reasons and environmental protection issues. This paper confirms the research statement made in the initial proposal. The present PhD research fills the gap in the scholarly literature dealing with the liability regime of the multimodal carrier; it completes the three comprehensive and analytic treatises in multimodal transport law, namely **"Multimodal Transport: Carrier Liability and Documentation"[69]**, **"Multimodal**

---

[67] McDOWELL (CARL E.), Op. Cit, p.p.: 503-513; Hazelwood (Steven J.), ***P&I CLUBS LAW AND PRACTICE,*** Third Edition, LLP, p.p. 176-210

[68] Bennett (Howard), The Law of Marine Insurance, Oxford, 1996; Hazelwood (Steven J.) ..., P&I Clubs: Law And Practice, 4th Edition, LLP, 2010; McDOWELL (Carl E.), Op. Cit., p.p.: 503-512; Rhidian (D), The Modern Law of Marine Insurance, Volume 3, Informa, London, 2009; The Right Honourable Lord Justice Mance Iain Goldrein, QC Professor Robert Merkin, Insurance Disputes, 2nd Edition, LLP, London & Hong Kong, 2003

[69] De Wit (Ralph), ***Multimodal Transport: Carrier Liability and Documentation***, Lloyd's of London 1995

Transport Law: The law applicable to the multimodal contract for the carriage of goods,"[70] and "Multimodal Transport Rules"[71]

In addition to that, it adds to the available literature on Multimodal Transport Law a comprehensive and analytic research on the Protection and Indemnity Insurance.

Hence the contribution of the research study to the promotion of International Trade through Harmonization and Standardization of rules related to the multimodal transportation mode and designing adequate insurance covers.

---

[70] Hoeks (Marian), *Multimodal Transport Law: The Law applicable to the multimodal contract for the carriage of goods,* 2010

[71] Kindred (H. M) & Brooks (M. R.), *Multimodal Transport Rules,* Kluwer Law International, Dordrecht, The Netherlands, 1997

Chapter III

Impact Of The International Intermodal Transportation On Current Insurance Schemes

The International trade plays a vital role in the global economy which is in a crucial need of ships and the overall shipping industry. Most of the products needed in our global economy are brought to their consumers by sea.[72] Nevertheless, despite the technical progress in shipping, the advent of the cellular containership and the progress achieved with regard to safety of ships, including progress in the area related to the protection of the marine environment, many casualties leading to significant loss of cargo occur in a much wider proportion than in the early days of shipping. With this enormous amount of cargo being moved all over the world, it is not surprising that more casualties occur at sea.

Insuring a vessel liability

It is estimated that the world merchant fleet exceeds 85,000 vessels with a combined gross tonnage of more than 1 billion GT (Gross tonnage).[73]

Marine cargo insurers provide cover for known quantifiable goods in favour of cargo owners.

Besides Cargo Insurance, there is also a need for ship owners to be protected against liability for loss or damage to cargo in carriage of goods.

This protection is generally offered through the legal institution of Protection and Indemnity insurance.

Shipping is still needed and this necessity for ships will continue to grow in the future.

Ship owners need to protect themselves against the risks associated with the seaborne trade and manage efficiently their ships.

---

[72] Chuah (Jason), *Law of International Trade,* Third Edition, Thomson *Sweet & Maxwell, p.p: 21-26

[73] IGP & I (International Group of P&I Clubs), ANNUAL REVIEW 2011/2012, page 3

The basic provisions in carriage of goods by sea are formulated at article 3 of the Hague-Visby Rules which is the equivalent of article ... in Hague Rules.[74]

Article 3, § 2, of the Hague-Visby Rules:

"Subject to the provisions of Article 4..., the carrier shall properly and carefully load, handle, stow, carry, keep care for and discharge the goods carried."...

This formulation was adapted at different periods of time in order to meet the ever changing conditions in carriage of goods from bulk shipping to cellular container ships through the general cargo shipments context.[75]

Failure for the maritime carrier to fulfil his main duties of taking care of cargo once the goods are loaded on the ship and delivering the goods in the same state and quantity as the goods loaded leads to the carrier being held liable in case of damage or loss to cargo according to the Hague Rules, Hague-Visby Rules and Hamburg Rules.

Except in the situations where the carrier is exonerated from his liability for damage to goods or loss of goods as enumerated in Article 4, the carrier should compensate the cargo owner in case of damage of goods under his care.

The newly adopted Rotterdam Rules[76] mention even the delay in delivery of goods as situation (cause) leading to the carrier´s liability.

Once damage to cargo (loss of cargo) has occurred and the carrier held liable for the damage, the cargo owner will need to be compensated for the damage. In practice, the cargo underwriter will pay the owner of the cargo. The cargo underwriter will then seek to recover his losses from the ship owner through subrogation.[77]

---

[74] Tetley (William), *Marine Cargo Claims*, Fourth Edition, Volume 1, THOSON *Carswell, 2008, p. 6; The Hague Rules stand for "International Convention for the Unification of Certain Rules of Law Relating to Bills of Lading, signed at Brussels, August 25, 1924 and in force as of June2, 1931;
The term "Hague-Visby Rules 1968" refers to the Hague Rules 1924, as amended by the "Protocol to Amend the International Convention for the Unification of Certain Rules of law Relating to Bills of Lading, adopted at Brussels, February 23, 1968, which Protocol entered into force June 23, 1977

[75] Tetley (William), *Op. Cit,* p-p 6-91 [Hague, Hague-Visby Rules and Hamburg Rules

[76] Formally, the United Nations Convention on Contracts for the International Carriage of Goods wholly or partly by Sea, 2008, United Nations. The convention is not yet into force

[77] The doctrine of subrogation states that the insurer may step into the shoes of the assured and enforce any claim, defence or set-off the assured possesses against any third party; this right arises only after that the insurer has paid for the loss.
For further details, please refer to the following:
Chuah (Jason), *Law of International Trade,* 3rd Edition, P.P.: 448-452

The ship owner will hand over the case of damage to his insurer who is a Protection & Indemnity Club known under the acronym "P&I Club."

One of the following international conventions shall determine the rules applicable to the damage:

Hague Rules (1924),

Hague-Visby Rules (1968) and

Hamburg Rules (1978).[78]

In addition to the aforementioned maritime liability regimes, it would be relevant to name

The Rotterdam Rules which will be studied in relation to the risks generally covered in Protection & Indemnity Marine Insurance.

In the present section, the maritime liability regimes are assessed against their impact on marine insurance law & Practice.

It is assumed that no party involved in cargo claims can master all the legal complexity around the question dealing with the ship owner's liability with its impact in the insurance industry. Another challenge will be about the removal of the "vacuum areas" with regard to the insurance of loss of goods in seaborne trade. The analysis of marine claims will illustrate some difficulties in this respect.

Therefore, the paper is restricted to the following issues: compensation of damages, limitation of liability, notification of the damage to cargo (cargo loss), time limitation of action (effect of the Time-Bar) and the impact of the Rotterdam Rules on the marine insurance industry. Since the liability of the ship owner is covered by the P & I Insurance Policy, what role will be played by Cargo Insurance? Is Cargo Insurance still needed in the International Seaborne Trade?

Some words on the Marine Insurance Industry

The present section will enhance the understanding of the subject. Two main aspects of insurance are considered here: third party liability for cargo claims offered in Protection & Indemnity marine insurance (P & I) and Cargo Insurance which is offered on the open market of insurance.[79]

In order to present a complete picture of insurance schemes in respect of the International Intermodal Carriage of Goods damages caused by ships at intersection of the various transportation segments (in port areas) and damages occurring to cargoes in transit should be considered.

---

[78] United Nations Convention on the carriage of Goods by Sea, signed at Hamburg on March 31, 1978, and in force November 1, 1992

[79] Hodge (Susan), *Cases and Materials on Marine Insurance Law,* Cavendish Publishing Limited (London-Sydney), p.p. 1-2, 2002

London is still the most important centre of the marine insurance market in the world. Nevertheless, there are some other growing insurance centres in Scandinavia with development in Oslo, New York, Paris, Hamburg and Tokyo.

Lloyd's of London needs to be mentioned; it is a unique and interesting body marked by the British maritime heritage. It started in Edward Lloyd's coffee house (1688). This was a meeting place where ship owners and traders met to discuss commercial transactions. Individual merchants would accept part of the risk of the shipping and underwrite their signature on a police of insurance. A committee was set up in order to supervise the transactions in 1771. In 1871 Lloyd's was incorporated by a Parliament Act. Basically, the system is still the same.[80]

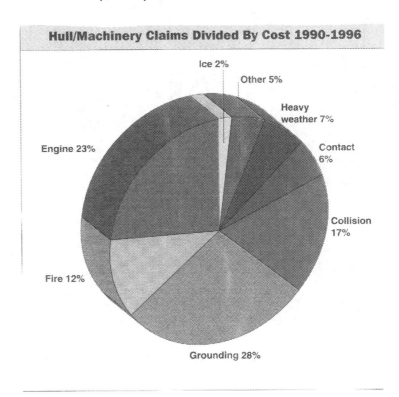

The Swedish Club

on their

125th Anniversary

---

[80] Alderton (P. M.), *Sea Transport: Operation and Economics,* London, Thomas Reed Publications Ltd, 1984, p.-p. 205-207

Lloyd´s is the world´s leading insurance market market where almost anything can be insured: fleet of ships and aircraft, communications satellites, super tankers, civil engineering projects, factories, oil rigs, refineries, livestock and nuclear power stations to name just a few of the thousand-and-one risks arising from the various fields of human activities and development in technology. This business flows to Lloyd´s from all parts of the world.

Lloyd´s is a society of underwriters, all of whom accept insurance risks for their personal profit or loss and who are liable to the full extent of their private fortunes for compensation of insurance risks. The merchant of the past signing, or underwriting, insurance policies in the coffee house incidental to his main business, led a long time ago to the professional underwriter employed by others to accept business at Lloyd´s on their behalf. The members of Lloyd´s are grouped into 400 syndicates of various sizes. The placing of a risk requires negotiations between the Lloyd´s broker and the underwriter. Here is one of the basic principles, namely: spreading the risk as widely as possible among syndicates in order to solve even heavy insurance claims.

Underwriters at Lloyd´s have no contact with the insuring public and their premium income entirely depends on the initiative and enterprise of Lloyd´s brokers in obtaining business throughout the world. The Council of Lloyd´s demands the highest professional standards from the companies of accredited Lloyd´s brokers allowed to placing risks at Lloyd´s. The prime duty of Lloyd´s brokers is to negotiate the best available deals for their customers.

For this purpose they have freedom to place risks wherever they think fit, whether at Lloyd´s, with insurance companies, or both.

In 1986, the market moved to its new headquarters, the eighth home in its 300 year history.

Nowhere in the world could be found so much underwriting expertise under one roof as at Lloyd´s. Although syndicates compete with each other, they also share expertise between themselves. The innovative infrastructure and the high level of security for its policyholders make Lloyd´s a unique market in the business world.[81]

In their new building the underwriters maintain their tradition by sitting in "boxes" reminding the old coffee tables of the old coffee house. Lloyd´s of London is a vast insurance market place where an insurance broker representing the ship owner move among the underwriters with a request to accept part of the risk. When they accept the risk they sign the ´slip´, indicating the part of the risk they are ready to accept. From the slip the policy, the insurance contract, is established.

Lloyd´s is not a company: it is defined as a collection of individuals who have agreed to accept the commercial discipline and code of conduct established by the committee of Lloyd´s.[82]

---

[81] Author´s Report on study visit at Lloyd´s of London (Personal Record), May 2013

[82] Author´s Report on study visit at Llod´s of London (Personal Record), May 2013

Cargo Insurance

The primary function of Cargo Insurance is indemnification of claimants for proven loss of cargo or damage to goods.

Cargo insurance helps protect the interest of the shipper and keep transport costs to a minimum. Its main advantage is that it can be exactly tailored to meet the requirements of the shipper with regard to the transportation risks covered and the sums insured.[83]

It is worth noting that in any export/import contract consideration should be given to the relationship between the insurance cover and the sale contract.

Intermodal Carriage of Goods plays a vital role in International Trade and cargo insurance facilitates trades by providing a risk distribution mechanism. The cargo owner would normally expect that insurance will act as an effective risk distribution mechanism only if it provides full and complete cover from the moment goods are placed at the care of the carrier until they are delivered.

Goods are insured by using the following Standard Insurance Clauses:

* ★ Institute Cargo Clauses (ICC), 1982 and 2009 versions

* ★ Institute Cargo Clauses (Air), 1982 and 2009 versions

* ★ Inland Transit Clauses drafted by various insurers.

The common feature in such policies is the fact that they provide cover from warehouse to warehouse (Transit Clause cl. 8 in ICC 1982 and 2009 and cl 5 in ICC (Air) 1982 and cl. 6 in ICC (Air) 2009.

The Transit Clause deals with the Attachment of Risk. This means those risks related to the goods leaving the warehouse.[84]

The Standard Insurance Clauses do not provide complete cover in the context of Intermodal Carriage of Goods. Therefore, tailor-made clauses are often used to supplement ICC and ICC (Air). They are known as "voyage clauses".

This is formulated in the following terms: "Cover attaches from the time the carrier accepts the delivery of the goods and continues during the transit".

---

[83] Vitiritti (Luis), ´Zurich Marine Risk Insight 2011´, Insights in Marine Risk, June 2011, p. 2; McDowell (Carl E.), `Containerization: Comments on Insurance and Liability´, 3 JML & C. 500 1971-1972 (HeinOnline), p.p. 509-512

[84] Author´s Report on study visit at Lloyd´s of London (Personal Record), May 2013

It is argued that Cargo Insurance, with respect to losses and damages for which carriers are responsible, is a banking service, in the sense that the cargo owner receives the funds promptly and remains in business with a minimal disruption of their business without using their own financial resources or credit. In contrast with the compensation mechanism in Cargo Insurance, the present system dealing with carriers´ liability often does not provide a prompt compensation.[85]

Thus, it can be concluded that Cargo Insurance has a positive impact on the development of the International Trade.

Protection and Indemnity Marine Insurance

P&I Insurance has traditionally been provided by mutual ship owners´ associations called "P&I Clubs" which appeared in the 1850´s. The Clubs are mutual insurance associations of which the ship owners are members. They are owned by, and run for the benefit of their members.

In contrast with commercial marine insurers who are answerable to their shareholders, the clubs are run as non-profit-making businesses.[86] The Group Clubs compete between themselves. Nevertheless, they share between them liabilities in excess of 8 million US Dollars up to a maximum limit of around 7 billion Dollars through the structure of the International Group Agreement.

The International Group basically performs three key functions: the operation of the claims pooling and reinsurance programme, providing a forum for the exchange and consideration of views on issues relating to ship owners´ marine liabilities and insurance arrangements, as well as external representation.[87]

As to the general financial situation related to P&I Clubs, the following trend has been observed.[88]

---

[85] Hodges (Susan), *Op. Cit.,* p.p. 87-99; McDOWELL (Carl E.), *Op. Cit.,* p.p. 509-510.
In addition, it should be noted that "The Institute Cargo Clauses (A), (B) and (C) are of particular relevance here.

[86] IGP&I, Op. Cit. P. 3

[87] IGP & I, Op. Cit. P. 3; Alderton (P. M.), *Sea Transport: Operation and Economics,* London and Sunderland, Thomas Reed Publications Ltd, 1984, p. p. 206-207

[88] Frank (Jerry), ´North of England, a winner in annual renewals´, Lloydslist.com, 20-02-2009

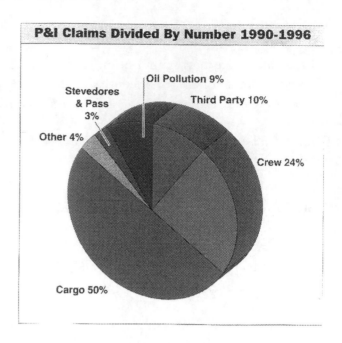

P&I Claims Divided By Number 1990-1996

Oil Pollution 9%

Third Party 10%

Stevedores
& Pass
3%

Other 4%

Crew 24%

Cargo 50%

The Swedish Club

on their

125th Anniversary

A few clubs reported an underwriting surplus and the risks have been both increasing and getting more complex due to new requirements in relation to the environmental protection and the need for more safety, including providing more security in maritime transportation fields. Facing the economic crisis in 2008, many clubs experienced financial difficulties with their reserves going significantly down: except the North of England, the Newcastle based Protection & Indemnity Club and Gaard (in Norway), most of the clubs had to settle very high claims.

Moreover, the entered tonnages (insured ships) were getting older and, as a result of that, many more damages occurred. However, the prevailing situation in 2009 was characterized by a financial recovery that has been taking place in the Insurance Industry until now. The International Group of P & I Clubs has been pursuing general increases of between 12.5% and 29% while members were struggling with the sharp decrease in the freight and financial market.

As an illustration of the described situation, six of the mutuals- American, London, Steamship, The Swedish Club, UK and The West of England – made unbudgeted call as pressure in the financial market reduced their investments portfolios (financial reserves).

The following two years have been marked by recovery and stability in the marine insurance industry.

A new trend with particular relevance to P&I mutual insurance is both the advent of "Independent P&I Clubs" in the newly industrialised countries (Brazil, China, India and South Korea) and the presence of "The Commercial Insurers of P&I Liabilities." These new comers are offering worthy P&I insurance covers.

The presence of these independent actors and high competition coming from Commercial P&I facilities and other insurance schemes more suitable to the new trends in the transportation industry provided on the commercial marked have increased the level of competition associated with the P&I insurance which is moving from a situation of oligopoly to a fairly open market.

LEGAL IMPACTS

1. Compensation of damage: calculation and type of damage

The three maritime carrier liability conventions were adopted at different periods of time and were conceived differently in respect of the concept of damages and the methods of damage evaluation.[89]

The Hague-Visby Rules contain some instructions on the calculation of damages. In spite of these instructions, it could be difficult to get their real meaning, for example Article 5 (b) of the Hague-Visby Rules. What is the meaning of the sentence "...Total amount recoverable shall be calculated by reference to the value of such goods at the place and time at which the goods are discharged..."

The Report of the President of the Commission suggests that the mentioned article simply lays down a "Prima Facie" measure of damages. This means that damages have to be assessed according to the appropriate circumstances and can include the recovery of additional damages.

Taking a quick look at the question dealing with additional damages, it leads to controversy.[90]

---

[89] Bauer (R. Glenn), ´Conflicting Liability Regimes: Hague-Visby v. Hamburg Rules – A Case by Case Analysis´ p. 53, HeinOnline – 24 JML & Com. 53 1993; Hoeks (Marian), *Multimodal Transport Law: The Law applicable to the multimodal contract for the carriage of goods,* p.p. 81-85, 2010

[90] Von Ziegler (Alexander), ´Compensation of Damage´, Paper presented at the conference on the Rotterdam Rules, Rotterdam, The 24th of September 2009 (Concept of financial impact of the Loss).

However, most jurisdictions and good practice in insurance generally assess the real circumstances and if, found appropriate, should be included in the recoverable amount.

In the Hamburg Rules, the matter is left to the applicable law. The main issue here will be how to find this applicable law knowing the difficult context of the carriage of goods regimes.

What about the Rotterdam Rules (RR)?

RR, Article 22 (3): The provisions can be understood as clarification that no further weight or items are considered unless agreed.

Research on relevant cases shows that cases are decided in the spirit of considering all potential and possible claims in the restrictive rules of the carriage conventions.[91]

2. Limitation of liability

Limitation of liability is inherent to the international seaborne trade. It was conceived in order to encourage owners to engage their resources (Crew members and sea-going ships) in carriage of goods in spite of the many hazards of the sea and protect them from unlimited exposure to liability. It is important to note the variation of limits in the maritime liability regimes with package limit and weight limit.

With regard to package limit, the amount per convention is as follows: 666.67 in Hague-Visby Rules, 835 in Hamburg Rules and 875 in the Rotterdam Rules. Taking into account the weight limit, the distribution is illustrated in this way: 2 in Hague/Hague-Visby Rules, 2.5 in Hamburg Rules and 3 in the Rotterdam Rules.[92]

A legal issue of great interest is the discussion as to whether a container is a package or the goods contained therein are packages.

Courts interpreting the Hague Rules have had difficulty in assessing whether a container should be a package for the purpose of limitation of liability. It generally depends on the descriptions in the bill of lading. In case the bill of lading describes the container as one package without listing its contents, the container itself is the package.

However, in the case where the bill of lading includes a reference to the contents inside the container, the contents determine the number of packages. According to Article 2 (C) of Hague-Visby Rules, the container will be a package or unit if the number of packages or units inside is not enumerated in the bill of lading.[93]

---

[91] Tetley (W), Op. Cit; Hazelwood (Steven J.), *P&I CLUB, Law and Practice*, 2010

[92] Von Ziegler (Alexander), ´Compensation of Damage´, Paper presented at the conference on the Rotterdam Rules, Rotterdam, 24 September 2009

[93] Tetley (W), Op. Cit, p.p. 1543-1545 (with report of relevant cases in various jurisdictions)

The Rotterdam Rules address this issue at Article 59 and the principle of solution is the following: *"The packages or shipping units enumerated in the contract particulars as packed in containers or pallets are deemed packages or shipping units."*

Another concern with respect to the container in the wake of damages due to defective lashing systems leading to very costly maritime disasters is to assess whether a slot charterer is entitled to the same limitation of liability as the ship owner. In Metvale Ltd v. Monsato International and others, Mr Justice Teare decided that slot charterers were entitled to limit liability under the convention.[94]

SKULD, ONE HUNDRED YEARS

OSLO, 1997

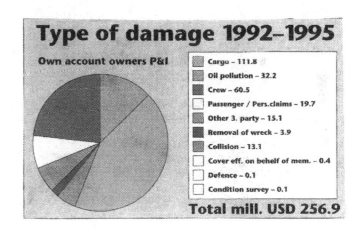

As to the validity of limitation clauses of liability, these clauses are not accepted in case the damage or loss has occurred by negligence from the carrier.[95]

3. Notice of damage

Notification of damage to the carrier is a prerequisite to any claim from a breach of contract in Carriage of Goods. Failure from the consignee or the shipper to give timely notice of damage to the carrier may result in the loss of the rights for compensation. The rules dealing with the

---

[94] Please, read also Hjalmarsson (Johanna), ´Shipping & Trade Law´, 2009, (2), 3-4

[95] Case 515 US 528, 115 S. Ct, 23 22, 132 L. Ed. 2nd 462-Supreme Court-Google Scholar: Loss of right to limitation of liability for ship owner´s negligence

notice of damage vary according to the different conventions. It is required from the shipper or the consignee to give a notice of loss or damage in writing to the carrier or his agent at the port of discharge before or at the time of the removal of the goods into the custody of the person entitled to delivery according to the contract of carriage in accordance with both the Hague and the Hague-Visby Rules.

In case the loss or damage is not apparent, the notice should be given within three days of delivery. There is no need for notice of damage in the case where the state of the goods has been subject of joint survey or inspection at the time of their reception.[96]

In the Hamburg Rules, the notice of loss or damage is specified at article 19. The notice should be given in writing by the consignee to the carrier not later than the working day after the day when the goods were handed over to the consignee.

As far as the Rotterdam Rules are concerned, they are more explicit about damage notification: it should be given within 21 consecutive days after delivery of the delayed goods (Article 23, 4, RR). The content of the notice in cases of delay should consist of:

* the information on delay (as damage) and

* the precision that the damage results from the delay.

Besides the damage notification, there is a delay within which a claim may be made against the carrier.

4. Limitation of Action–Effect of the Time Bar

In application of the Hague and Hague-Visby Rules, the time-bar limit related to claims against the maritime carrier with regard to liability for loss of good or damage to goods is one year (Article 3). In the case of any actual or apprehended loss or damage, the carrier and the consignee (shipper) should give all reasonable facilities to each other for inspecting and tallying the goods.[97]

In the Hamburg Rules the delay for claims has been fixed to two years (Article 20). In addition to this principle, the person against whom a claim is made may at any time during the running of the limitation period extend that period by a declaration in writing to the claimant. The period can be further extended by another declaration or declarations.[98] These provisions are very often used by both parties once a marine cargo claim has been introduced. In that regard, careful attention should be given to all the documents exchanged between parties for the delay extension.[99]

---

[96] Article III (9) of Hague-Visby Rules

[97] Article III (5) of Hague-Visby Rules

[98] Article III (5) of Hague-Visby Rules

[99] As Standard Rule of practice in P&I Insurance

Cases

It was held in "Aries Tanker Corp. V Total Transport Ltd" that the carrier was discharged from all liability in application of the rules on Limitation of Action in Hague-Visby Rules.[100]

This principle was confirmed later in the case "Bua International Ltd v Hai Hing Shipping Co Ltd.[101]

The principle that the limitation period applies regardless of whether the claim is founded in tort or contract is found in the case Salmond and Spraggon (Australia) Pty Ltd v Port Jackson Stevedoring.[102]

5. Implications of the Rotterdam Rules in P&I Insurance and Cargo Insurance

The newly adopted Convention on Contracts for the International Carriage of Goods Wholly or Partly by Sea which is also called "Maritime Plus" instrument is intended to replace the three existing conventions relating to the ship owner liability.

In spite of the desirability of the rules established in the new convention, there is no unanimity as to the future effectiveness of the rules.

P&I Clubs are of the general opinion that the rules may add some extra costs in marine insurance.[103] Nevertheless, they believe that a single liability regime would speed claims payments and reduce claims costs in the long term: a single standard should reduce uncertainty and enable claims to be settled faster.

The rules are largely debated by practitioners, legal experts and scholars with deep insights in issues relating to the harmonization of the rules associated with the Carriage of Goods and Marine Insurance Law & Practice.[104]

Before engaging in the discussion and arguments pertaining to the need and viability of the adopted convention, it is advisable to identify the specific provisions in the Rotterdam Rules relevant to global challenges that need to be addressed in the future development of the Insurance Industry. These rules are designed to regulate both the International Maritime Carriage of Goods and the International Multimodal Carriage of Goods including a sea leg.

---

[100] The Aries (1977) 1, Lloyd´s Rep. 334, by the House of Lords

[101] The Hai Hing (2000) 1, Lloyd´s Rep. 300

[102] The New York Star, (1980) 2, Lloyd´s Rep. 317

[103] This has always been the position of the P&I Clubs during the process of elaboration of the Rotterdam Rules.

[104] D. Rhidian (Thomas), ´And then there were the Rotterdam Rules´, (2008) 14 JIML, p.p. 189-190; Eftestol-Wilhelmsson (Ellen), ´The Rotterdam Rules in a European Context´, (2010), 16 JML

The terms "A Maritime Plus Instrument" refer to the new technology in the Convention, changes to some traditional terminology and familiar terms (For example, "Bills of Lading" and "Sea Waybills" are now included in the general terms "Transport Documents" in the Rotterdam Rules.

Then, what can be the consequence of a possible ratification of the Convention in Cargo Claims?

It is argued that ratification will significantly increase the liability of ship owners and maritime carriers in respect of the International Carriage of Goods regime. In particular, the long established exception related to the error in the navigation or management of the ship (the nautical fault exception) would be excluded. The obligation to exercise due diligence and to provide a seaworthy ship has been extended to the duration of the voyage instead of being restricted to before and at the commencement of the voyage as specified in the Hague/Hague-Visby Rules.[105]

The limits of liability per package or unit of weight have been significantly increased beyond Hague-Visby and Hamburg Rules limits. The liability of the owners and other maritime carriers for the negligence of maritime performing parties would be regulated by the Rules.[106] It should be mentioned here that the NVOOC (Non vessel Owning Operating Companies) are considered as Maritime Carriers.

At present, it is not possible to evaluate the economic impact of these increased liabilities, but it is obvious to mention that ship owners and their P&I insurers would see a significant increase in the cost of cargo claims in case the Rotterdam Rules are globally adopted.

Nevertheless, the convention contains a number of new and effective features. The scope of application of the convention would extend to door-to-door carriage and tackle-to-tackle/ port-to-port carriage and many of the beneficial aspects of existing conventions and regimes are retained.

In particular, it retains the existing concept of network liability, whereby liability and the applicable limits of liability for loss of and damage to the goods occurring before or after the sea-leg will be a matter of any unimodal international instrument compulsory applicable to the relevant mode of transport where the loss or damage occurs.

The Rotterdam Rules retain the concept of fault-based liability found in the hague/Hague-Visby Rules, but the standards and burdens of proof overall are more onerous for the carrier. The convention has provisions for electronic commerce. It also allows more freedom of contract in the liner trade by introducing the concept of "Volume Contract" in International Carriage of Goods.

Similarly to the existing conventions, the Rotterdam Rules would apply to transport documents, such as bills of lading and sea waybills, issued both in liner and in non–liner trades.

---

[105] Rotterdam Rules as seen by the P&I CLUB West of England, Luxemboug, Review, 2012

[106] This can be seen through comparison of art. 4 (5) of Hague, Article 45 (5a) of Hague-Visby Rules, Article 6 (1a) of Hamburg Rules and Article 59 (1) of Rotterdam Rules

The Rotterdam Rules address the issues dealing with jurisdictions and arbitration: the relevant provisions are essentially based on the restrictive approach of the Hamburg Rules. Under the Rules, cargo owners can effectively choose from a number of jurisdictions the court where they can sue the carrier.

As to the exclusive jurisdiction agreements contained often in contracts of carriage, they do not have primacy. However, these provisions are subject to an "opt in" by States.[107] The ability of cargo owners to choose from a number of jurisdictions may lead to greater uncertainty for carriers and insurers and high costs due to the fact that courts in countries unfamiliar with such complex issues are asked to decide test cases arising under the Convention.

As it appears, the Rotterdam, Rules seem to be an ambitious project trying to codify many aspects of carriage of goods by sea. There seems little doubt that the statu quo of existing regimes will not remain in case of no ratification of the Rules: the EU and the United States would enact their own domestic legislation.

While advising the International Group of P&I Clubs (IG), the International Chamber of Shipping (ICS) and the European Community Ship Owners´Associations (ECSA), the European Commission indicated that they remain open minded with regard to the question of the desirability of a European multimodal convention. The European Commission has publicly criticized the Rotterdam Rules. The reason for that is that the rules do not conform to European multimodal expectations.[108]

Generally speaking, it should be desirable that the Rotterdam Rules enter into force. The number of ratifications required for that has been set at twenty.

If the Rotterdam Rules can have any real impact, it will need to be adopted by a large number of States. Therefore, it can be mentioned here as an example that approximately 90 States ratified the Hague/Hague-Visby Rules but only 34 ratified the Hamburg Rules. Among the 34 States which ratify the Hamburg Rules there were no major trading nations in seaborne trade.

Standard for Protection and Indemnity Cover

Club cover for liability in respect of cargo is based on the relevant contract of carriage which is subject to terms no less favourable than the limits in the Hague/Hague-Visby Rules. The Club´s Cargo Standard Rule generally provides as follows:

"... there is no cover in respect of liabilities which would not have been payable by the Member if the contract of carriage had incorporated the Hague/Hague-Visby Rules, or similar rights, immunities and limitations in favour of the Carrier. There is no cover in respect of liabilities

---

[107] The Rotterdam Rules as seen by the P&I CLUB West of England, Luxembourg, Review, 2012

[108] The Rotterdam Rules as seen by the P&I CLUB West of England, Luxembourg, Review, 2012

arising under the Hamburg Rules unless the Hamburg Rules are compulsorily applicable to the contract of carriage by operation of law."[109]

Club cargo cover is based on the liability regime set out in the Hague/Hague-Visby Rules mainly because it is recognized that this has been the accepted standard for a long time, standard according to which the majority of ship owners and cargo owners contract commercially, when contractual terms are not imposed by law.

Besides, the Hague Rules in the case of the USA and Hague-Visby Rules with regard to other major trading States have been adopted as ground for domestic legislation. It is worth remembering that when the Hamburg Rules came into force, the clubs did not substitute them for the Hague/Hague-Visby Rules. The reasons for that are that those States which had ratified the Convention are not major trading nations and the industry was not interested in the Hamburg Rules.[110]

The legal issue which would inevitably arise is as follows:

To what extent P&I Cover should be available for liabilities incurred by Members in the context of the Rotterdam Rules being ratified?

The provisions of the new Convention would normally become compulsorily applicable by law in the relevant State where that State either ratifies the Convention and the Convention has entered into force or enacts its provisions by other means into its domestic law (for example, the US COGSA).

Hence, the Club would indemnify a member in respect of cargo liabilities arising compulsorily by law under the new Convention. However, if the member had voluntarily agreed to the incorporation of the Rotterdam Rules into the contract of carriage, the position of the Club would be different: the Club would not cover liabilities arising under the Rotterdam Rules in excess of those which would be covered according to the Hague/Hague-Visby Rules.

At present, there is uncertainty about the future of the Rotterdam Rules.

Would the major maritime trading countries ratify the new Convention?

If they do ratify these rules, would they incorporate all the rules into their domestic law?

Many scholars have been discussing the aforementioned questions; it seems advisable to mention some studies of relevance.[111]

---

[109] Standard Rule in P&I Marine Insurance

[110] The main maritime trading countries still prefer the maritime carrier liability regime established in the Hague-Visby Rules

[111] Eftestol-Wilhelmsson (Ellen), ´The Rotterdam Rules in a European Multimodal Context´, (2010), 16 JML; D. Rhidian (Thomas), ´And then there were the Rotterdam Rules´, (2008), 14 JIML, pp. 189-190

In addition to that, it remains to be seen to what extent carriers will be willing to adopt the Rotterdam Rules as the standard for their carriage terms, and, with particular reference to the marine insurance industry. There might be differing opinions from those engaged in liner shipping as opposed to other sectors.

Another uncertainty factor is the position of the International P&I Group. It is not presently known whether and, if so, when the Group Clubs will consider it appropriate to replace the Hague/Hague-Visby Rules with the Rotterdam Rules as the standard for P&I Cover after ratification of the Rules. The views of the Clubs´ membership as a whole will be a determinant factor in the process of the voluntary incorporation of the Rotterdam Rules in the contract of carriage. It is highly suggested that the Clubs keep the matter under regular review.[112]

As to the current situation, a Member who is in need to be covered for liabilities which he has voluntarily accepted and agreed beyond the normal standard of the Hague/Hague-Visby Rules may ask his Club to arrange cover for the additional liabilities on special terms by agreement (Here is an affirmation of the principle of Freedom of Contract tailored to the need of the Member).[113]

Conclusion (Chapter III)

The Standard Club Cargo Cover is currently based on the liability regime set out in the Hague/Hague-Visby Rules: these rules have been recognized for a long time ago as the accepted standard according to which the majority of maritime carriers and cargo owners contract commercially when contractual terms are not imposed by law. Another factor in favour of the Hague/Hague-Visby regimes lies in the ratification or adoption of these rules as the basis for domestic legislation by a significant number of States, including the major trading nations.

Insofar, the marine insurance industry has been reluctant to adopt the Hamburg Rules as standard regime in Third Party liability and in Cargo Insurance. As to the Rotterdam Rules, they are not yet into force; there is uncertainty on whether, if ratified, they can be adopted as standard in the Marine Insurance Industry. Nevertheless, the rules can contribute to a substantial reduction in claims in virtue of harmonisation of the rules relating to the carriage of goods by sea in a single regime in the long run.

Currently, a maritime carrier or a cargo owner can afford the needed insurance cover by agreement with the insurance provider.

---

[112] IGP&I, Op. Cit. Pp: 4-11

[113] Standard Rule in P&I Marine Insurance

BIBLIOGRAPHY ON CARRIER'S LIABILITY & INSURANCE SCHEMES

Textbooks

Chua (Jason), *Law of International Trade,* Third Edition, Thomson Sweet & Maxwell, London 2005

Hazelwood (Steven J.), *P&I Club: Law and Practice,* 2010

Hodges (Suan), *Cases and Materials on Marine Insurance Law,* Cavendish, London-Sydney, 2002

Hoeks (Marian), *Multimodal Transport Law: The Law applicable to the Multimodal*

contract for the carriage of goods, 2010

Tetley (William), *Marine Cargo Claims,* Fourth Edition, Volume 1, Thomson ★Carswell. 2008

Tetley (William), *Marine Cargo Claims,* Fourth Edition, Volume 2, Thomson ★Carswell, 2008

Review and Journal's Articles

Bauer (R. Glenn), ´Conflicting Liability Regimes: Hague – Visby v. Hamburg Rules – A case by Case Analysis´, 24 JML & Com. 531

Crowley (ME) – Tul. L. Rev. 2005, ´The Uniqueness of Admiralty and Maritime Law: The Limited Scope of the Cargo Liability Regime covering Carriage of Goods, Multimodal Transport´, 2005

D. Rhidian (Thomas), `And then there were the Rotterdam Rules´, (2008), JIML

Derrington (Sarah), ´Marine Insurance Act 1906 – Introduction´, Home Page www.findlaw.com.au (Article), 12/04/2012

Eftestol – Wilhelmsson (Ellen), `The Rotterdam Rules in a European Context´, (2010), 16 JIML

IGP&I (International Group of P&I Clubs), ´Annual Review`, 2011 – 2012, London

McDowell (Carl E.), `Containerization: Comment on Insurance and Liability´, 3. JML & C 500, 1971 – 1972

Vitiritti (Luis), ´Zurich Marine Risks, Insight´, 2011, Zurich

Rosaeg (E), ´The Applicability of Conventions for the Carriage of Goods and for Multimodal Transport´, Lloyd´s Maritime and Commercial Law Quaterly, 2002

Conference papers

Von Ziegler (Alexander), ´Compensatiopn of Damage´, Paper presented at the Conference on the Rotterdam, The 24th of Septembre 2009

Chapter IV

Case Study On The International Intermodal Transportation

Here is an analytic review associated with three major casualties involving Intermodal Transportation. It provides readers with an accurate idea of this mode of transport and gives an account of measures and recommendations which have been conceived by experts in order to promote and raise the level of security in International Trade. The following cases have been selected:

* MSC Napoli, The English Channel (the 18th of January 2007)

* NORFOLK SOUTHERN RAILWAY Co. V. JAMES N. KIRBY, Pty Ltd and

* KAWASAKI v. REGAL-BELOIT

"MSC NAPOLI" CASE

The English Channel, the 18th of January 2007

The Facts of the Case[114][115]

In the morning on the 18th of January 2007, the 4,419 TEUs container ship MSC Napoli was sailing in heavy seas, causing the ship to pitch heavily. The ship was making a speed of 11 knots when she suffered a catastrophic failure of her hull at the level of the engine room. Having assessed the gravity of the situation, the master promptly decided to abandon the ship.

The distress call was made and the 26 crew members immediately embarked on an enclosed lifeboat. They were rescued later by two Royal Navy helicopters. No staff member was injured. Afterwards, the ship was towed towards Portland, UK.

Due to the fact that the disabled vessel approaching the English Coast was at the apparent risk of breaking up or sinking, it was intentionally beached in Branscombe Bay on the 20th of January 2007. As a consequence, 114 boxes were lost overboard before the vessel listed heavily after beaching. The following factors which contributed to the failure of the hull structure were identified:

* The vessel´s hull did not have sufficient buckling strength in the areas of the engine room,

* The classification rules applicable at the time of the vessel´s construction did not require buckling strength calculations to be undertaken beyond the vessel´s amidships area,

* There was shortage of safety margin between the hull´s design loading and the ultimate strength,

* The load on the hull may have been increased by whipping effect, and finally,

* The ship´s speed exceeded the limit allowed in the heavy seas.

As measures of accidents prevention for other similar containerships, the MAIB requested the major classifications societies to conduct urgent evaluation on the buckling strength of a number of ship design.

As a result, over 1,500 ships were screened. Among them, 12 vessels have been identified as requiring remedial actions, a further 10 vessels were assessed as being borderline and requiring

---

[114] Hazelwood (Steven J.), *P&I CLUB, Law and Practice, 2010;*

[115] MAIB Casualty Report, `MSC NAPOLI´, (UK Registered Ship), Southampton, UK (Marine Accident Investigation Branch), SO 15 2DZ, Report Number 9/2008, April 2008

more detailed investigation. In addition, the screening of 8 container ships had to be done at the time of the report publication and remedial actions were undertaken.

Briefly, remedial actions were initiated and where necessary, operational limitations have been granted or strongly advised prior to the completion of the remedial work.

Recommendations were made to the International Association of Classification Societies (IACS) in order to increase the requirements for container ship design, consolidate current research into whipping effect and to initiate research into the development and use of technological aids for measuring hull stresses on container ships.

Assistance was requested from the International Chamber of Shipping for the purpose of promoting best practice in the operation of the container traffic. In all these actions attention was given to the improvement in safety management system adopted by shipping companies.

Litigation and Marine Insurance Issues116

Insurers of the 62,000-ton container ship which suffered a catastrophic hull failure have estimated the total bill for the wreck at British Pounds 120 million. The figure means the clean-up, the salvage, the vessel and the cargo costs are second only to the 2.1 billion dollars incurred by the EXXON Valdes; the tanker which split 10.8 million gallons of crude oil into the sea at Prince William Sound, Alaska, in 1989.[117]

The cost of the Napoli grounding was revealed by the London SteamShip Owners's Mutual Insurance Association. In its annual report, the Chief Executive Paul Hinton mentioned that the Napoli's pounds 120 million estimated bill was the "second most expensive claim ever." He added that the beaching of the vessel, which had 3.664 ton of fuel oil and marine diesel on board, had avoided "a potentially very grave environmental disaster."

He described the aftermath as "an enormous challenge in technical, regulatory and legal terms." The MSC Napoli represents the first occasion when almost the totality of a ship's container cargo has been brought ashore in both sound and extensively wetted condition for forwarding and disposal. (Extract from the Telegraph, the 7th 0f November 2008)

Financial Impact of the MSC Napoli Wreck

The London Steamship Owners Mutual Insurance Association revealed that the insurers estimate of the bill for the wreck, including the salvage operation, clean up, vessel and cargo cost amounted to 120 million British Pounds. This is the second highest wreck cost to date, next to the 2.1 billion USD cost incurred by the EXXON Valdez incident.

---

[116] Please note that additional information on the case can be found on the home page www.businessinsurance. com/article/20070123/News/20009313/msc-napoli, Online, the 1st of September 2016

[117] Report on the financial impact of the MSC Napoli wreck, 'The Telegraph', UK, the 7th of November 2008

The vessel salvage operation alone amounted to more than 50 million and Devon County Council spent 44,000 British Pounds on the clean up and a further amount of 320,000 British was spent on the operation by Devon and Cornwall Police and Fire services. The Municipal Authorities lost their money as they received roughly a third of what they spent from the insurance.

A marine lawyer handling the compensation claims advised that these claims (local claims) were in excess of 65 million Pounds. Under the Merchants Shipping Act 1995 ship owners and insurers are entitled to limit their liability.

In the MSC Napoli case, the limitation was fixed at 15 million Pounds: this was vastly under-estimation compensation which resulted in losses for all the involved parties.

"NORFOLK SOUTHERN RAILWAY Co. V. JAMES N. KIRBY, Pty ltd" CASE

In this case, a shipper contracted for transportation of cargo from Australia to a U.S. inland destination to a freight forwarder. The Supreme Court makes Inroads Promoting Uniformity and Maritime Commerce in Norfolk Southern Railway v. Kirby.[118]

Admiralty Jurisdiction in Mixed Contract Cases

Contemporary transport contracts, as in the case of a through bill of lading or a combined transport document encompass transport legs both by sea and by land. From a maritime perspective, jurisdiction over mixed contracts is not clear.[119]

Before Norfolk Southern Railway v. James N. Kirby, Pty Ltd, the rule was rather simply stated but not so easily applied. A mixed contract did not fall within admiralty jurisdiction, except in two circumstances:

★Where the dominant subject matter of the contract was maritime in nature and the land-based element was relatively minor or incidental to the transaction or

★Where the maritime segment and land-based segment were considered distinctively (severable).

Under the latter approach a court exercise jurisdiction over the maritime dispute, but it could not exercise jurisdiction over a dispute involving the land-based leg of the carriage.

The facts of the case120

The Kirby Case arose in the context of International Multimodal Carriage of Goods. Kirby desired to ship its products from its plant in Australia to its customer in Huntsville, Alabama. The firm entered into a contract with International Cargo Control (ICC) under which ICC would provide the carriage of goods under a "door to door" contract. ICC as freight forwarder made the arrangements for the transport of the goods, but did not actually perform the carriage.

ICC issued Kirby a "Through" bill of lading as proof of the contract of carriage of goods, which were packed in standard multimodal containers. According to this contract, ICC accepted liability as a carrier. Two provisions on limitation of damages were included in the ICC bill of lading. For any loss at sea the liability limit was the 500 USD per package limit. In addition, a Himalaya clause was incorporated into the shipping contract, but the parties negotiated a higher limitation

---

[118] Marva Jo Wyatt', 'COGSA Comes Ashore… And More', HeinOnline, 30 Tul. Mar. L.J 101 (2006)

[119] Force (Robert), 'The Aftermath of Norfolk Southern Railway v. James N. Kirby Pty Ltd: Jurisdiction and Choice of Law Issues', HeinOnline, 543 U.S. 14, 2004 AMC 2705 (2004) 1393

[120] Theis (H. William), 'Third-Party Beneficiary in Multimodal Contract of Carriage, Norfolk Southern Railway Co. v. James N. Kirby, Pty Ltd' 125 S. Ct. 385, 2004 AMC 2705 (2004), Journal of Maritime Law & Commerce 201 (2005)

rate for potential accidents arising during the inland leg of the journey (from Savannah, port areas, to Huntsville).

ICC's contract with Hamburg Sud to ship Kirby's equipment from Sydney to Savannah also adopted the COGSA limitation default of 500 U.S. Dollars per package. A Himalaya Clause extended the 500 Dollars per package limitation to all downstream carriers. Hamburg Sud arranged for the downstream carrier, Norfolk Southern, to complete the inland leg of the journey.

While the ocean part of the carriage was successfully performed, the Norfolk Southern train derailed en route to Huntsville, causing an estimated 1.5 million Dollars in damage to Kirby Equipment.

Principle of Solution

The essential question in "Kirby" was whether a contract, to which the maritime shipper was not a party, nevertheless limited the rights of that shipper against a land carrier, a railroad. The Supreme Court, in a unanimous opinion, protected the railroad. The Court's decision appears to support modern global thinking as it efficiently shifts the risks of cargo damage away from carriers by land or sea and their insurers on to shippers and their insurers.[121]

With the decision on this case about a train wreck begins the Supreme Court's remarkable opinion which turns out to be an important case about admiralty law. Kirby is important for the following reasons:

* It expands the Court's definition of admiralty jurisdiction,

* It extends the reach of judge- made admiralty law associated with the historic case of Southern much in the tradition Pacific Co. v. Jensen,

* It broadens the scope of protection given by admiralty law to third-party beneficiaries of contracts and

* It introduces an unusual approach to Agency Law whose field needs to be explored.[122]

---

[121] Sweeney (Joseph C.), ´Crossing the Himalayas: Exculpatory Clauses in Global Transport; Norfolk Southern Railway Co. v. James N. Kirby, Pty Ltd´, 125 S. Ct. 385, 2004 AMC 2705 (2004), Journal of Maritime Law & Commerce, Vol. 36, Number 2, April 2005

[122] Theis (William H.), 'Third-Party Beneficiaries in Multimodal Contracts of Carriage, Norfolk Southern Railway Co. v. James N. Kirby, Pty Ltd´, 125 S. Ct. 385, 2004 AMC 27 05 (2004), Journal of Maritime Law & Com 201 (2005), HeinOnline

"KAWASAKI KISEN KAISHA Ltd v. REGAL-BELOIT Corp." CASE

Exporting Import Litigation

According to the United States' Supreme Court's decision, the Carmack Amendment is not triggered when a domestic rail carrier accepts imported cargo.

The Carriage of Goods by Sea Act (COGSA) of 1936 can apply to both the Ocean and inland legs of a multimodal import shipment. For that reason, the Court's most recent decision gives further imprimatur to the use of Himalaya Clauses in through Ocean bills of lading to extend COGSA's application to subcontracting inland carriers who perform a part of the shipment's overall multimodal transportation.[123]

The legal issue associated with the applicable rule when goods are carried from a foreign port by sea and then inland by rail has been a concern among the Appeal courts in the United States.

More contentious has been the debate in situations where goods are carried according to a single contract which applies both to the sea and rail legs and also extends the application of maritime law to the entire carriage. The main question is formulated as follows: If the goods are damaged during the inland rail carriage, does federal rail-carrier law apply or does the contractually – extended Maritime Law apply?

The Supreme Court considered the provisions of through bill of lading, which purportedly extended the provisions of the Carriage of Goods by Sea Act (COGSA) to the Inland part of an International Multimodal Carriage.[124]

Facts of the Case

Shippers filed a claim against the ocean carrier and rail carrier which provides them with carriage of product from China to the United States in a California State Court to recover for damages. During the transport of the products, a train derailed damaging the goods. The case was removed to a California Federal District Court where it was dismissed under the ground that the contracts between the parties did not cover claims for cargo damages.

Afterwards, the U.S. Court of Appeal for the Ninth Circuit reviewed the District Court's decision. The court reasoned that the Carriage of Goods by Sea Act (COGSA) does not govern the inland leg of carriage, unless the parties opted out of coverage by the Carmack Amendment to Interstate Commerce Act. The Carmack Amendment regulates damage claims against motor and rail carriers, and restrictively limits the venues in which such suits could be filed.

---

[123] Commarano A. Dennis, 'Symposium – Impact of the Supreme Court Decision REGAL – BELOIT: EXPORTING IMPORT LITIGATION', 85 Tul. L. Rev. 1207 (2011)

[124] Abbott Marie (Jones), Berdy (Christopher), 'Defense Counsel Journal', 78.1 (JAN. 2011, 116-124

Given the fact that the District Court did not consider whether the parties opted out the COGSA by the Carmack, the Ninth Circuit (Court of Appeals) remanded the case for that determination.

Legal Issue

Does the Carmack Amendment apply to the inland segment of an international shipment?

No, the U.S. Supreme Court did not apply the Carmack Rules to the Regal-Beloit case: the rules are not appropriate when a domestic rail company accepts such imported cargo (from China). Instead, the Carriage of Goods by Sea Act (COGSA, 1936) can apply to both the Ocean and Inland legs of the International Intermodal import. Therefore, the case had to be assessed by a Chinese Court.

This is the consecration of the Himalaya Clause in Through Ocean Bills of Lading (A change to the Carmack Amendment).[125]

---

[125] Further reading for specialists can be found in the U.S. Supreme Court's materials under the case Kawasaki Kisen Kaisha Ltd. V. Regal-Beloit Corp./Union Pac. RR. V. Regal-Beloit Corp-AMICUS (Merits), Docket-number: Nos 08-1553 and 08-1554, Supreme Court Term: 2009 TERM; Court Level: U.S. Supreme Court

Conclusion

The continuous expansion of the International Intermodal Carriage of Goods has been observed since 1958 in the United States of America. The commercial consecration was marked by the arrival in Rotterdam of the container ship "Fairland" belonging to Sea-Land on the 3rd of May 1966. The ship sailed from New York for just a few days instead for weeks that used to take general cargo ships and bulk carriers.

The present book has been conceived as a milestone in this steady development in using standard boxes across the following transportation modes: shipping, railways, roads, airways and inland waterways. As any other technological innovation of commercial character Intermodal Transportation has led to many changes both in the Global Economy and Transport Infrastructure. The Carriage of Goods is currently considered as a transportation chain from the producer to the consumer. The book analyzes the essence of the concept of Intermodal Carriage of Goods, the adequate method of understanding the complexity of the Intermodal Transportation concept, the various Insurance Schemes associated with the Intermodal Carriage, the main legal challenges in intermodal Transportation and security, safety as well as environmental issues for the purpose of sustainability in the development of Transport.

Furthermore, the advent of "Dry Ports" or Terminal Containers all over the world marks a global development in the International Carriage of Goods.

Quintessence of the Intermodal Transportation Concept

Understanding the Intermodal Carriage of Goods is a requirement for people involved in International Trade at various levels, for example Municipal Authorities, Community Planners, policy makers and Industry investors. The whole philosophy behind the Intermodal Carriage of Goods is the packing of cargo into uniformly sized boxes (containers) and then designing all carrying vehicles such as trucks, railways and ships for the swift, safe and efficient transport of these boxes through the "door to door" concept.

Transportation technologies in the field of unitization of goods which culminated in the advent of containerization have led to the subsequent development of Intermodal Transport featured by the integration of the following modes of Carriage of Goods: Airways Carriage, Carriage by Sea, Inlands Waterways, Railways and Truck Services.

Whereas the technical, commercial and economic aspects of the International Intermodal Transportation have been adequately addressed in scholarly publications the legal regime associated with the liability of the Intermodal Carrier is still unpredictable, quite unreliable and does not respond to the requirements of the Intermodal Transportation for the purpose of the promotion of the Global Economy.

At present, transport in Carriage of Goods means getting goods delivered from the producer to the consumer: the process would more likely involve an International Intermodal Carriage. The unpredictable, inadequate and uncertain liability regime in International Carriage of Goods as referred to previously has a significant impact on the insurance schemes available in Intermodal Transportation.

As a consequence, the Insurance Industry has just been coping with conflicting laws and regulations while settling various claims arising from frequent and high capital-intensive risks in the International Intermodal Carriage of Goods.

Advantages and inconvenient of Intermodal Transportation

Among the advantages of using containers the following factors can be mentioned: faster cargo handling operations with economy in operations as one gang of twelve or fifteen men can discharge or load a 1,200 TEU- container ship within 24 hours, safety concerns with regard to breakage and pilferage, reducing packaging and the offer related to the door-to-door transport service.

Nevertheless, there are disadvantages in the use of containers: the traffic requires massive and intensive investments. Expensive container ships should be purchased and terminal infrastructures would need to be upgraded with computerized high speed cargo handling equipments. More skilled personnel should be trained in order to cope with the technical development. Further, the problem of an imbalance of trade in containerizable cargo leads to the unprofitable movement of empty containers. Introductory problems involving customs, documentation and conflicts of laws have been experienced.

Main Challenges associated with Intermodal Transportation

Six main challenges have been identified with regard to the expansion of Intermodal Transportation. They are:

* The economics of scale with the growing size of intermodal vehicles which contribute to casualties at sea and enormous pollutions in marine areas,

* There have been logistics problems to accommodate ships and to store goods in case of casualties involving larger container ships,

* Shortage of available contingency areas in coastal areas would need to be solved,

* The legal regime in Intermodal Transportation is still unreliable and unpredictable, leading to higher costs for litigation and impeding continuous growth in International Intermodal Carriage of Goods by limiting access to the benefits of its full potential;

* Technical issues in order to secure container ships stability and hull stress should be dealt with at international level.

* Human resources would require ongoing-training and more specialization in order to cope with technical and commercial innovations in Intermodal.

Statistical Data on Intermodal Transportation

Containerships Size Through The Years

1956: Ideal X-58 TEUs

1968: Encounter Bay-1,530 TEUs

1972: Hamburgh Express-2,950 TEUs

1980: Neptune Garnet-4,100 TEUs

1984: American New York-4,600 TEUs

1996: Regina Maersk-6,400 TEUs

1997: Susan Maersk-8,600 TEUs

2002: Charlotte Maersk-8,890 TEUs

2003: Anna Maersk-9,310 TEUs

2005: Gjertrud Maersk-10,500 TEUs

2006: Emma Maersk-11,000 TEUs

2012: Marco Polo (CMA CGM)-16,000 TEUs

2013: Maersk MC Kinney Moller-18,270 TEUs

2014: CSCL GLOBE-19,000 TEUs

Current studies show that the 6th Generation of Containerships represents a 1600% increase in TEU carrying capacity. The economics of scale in ships size lead to a viscous circle with ever increasing volumes yielding lower running costs.

The Panamax standard achieved in 1985 was about 4,000 TEUs. Post Panamax vessels have led to new configurations of networks and requirements for new handling equipment as well as increased berth depth at ports.

Furthermore, more storage areas are needed and ports hinterlands should need more adequate transport infrastructures.

Post New Panamax

By the year 2006 appear E Class Containerships with a carrying capacity in the range of 11,000–14,000 TEUs introduced by Maersk. Afterwards, the Triple E vessels or "Post New Panamax" were introduced into operations; these are bigger than the expanded Panama Canal specifications and can handle up to about 18,000 TEUs. There are designs on the drawing boards related to the "Malacca Max Class", Containerships that could carry about 27,000–30,000 TEUs. However, they are not expected to be constructed within a decade.

Containership Fleet–5,088 Vessels

1990 .... 1.5 million TEUs

2000 .... 4.3 million TEUs

2008 .... 10.6 million TEUs

2012 .... 16.3 million TEUs

2013 .... 17.3 million TEUs

2014 .... 19.0 million TEUs

2015 .... 20.7 million TEUs

Risk in Containership Operations

There is a potential of risk that can be evaluated to USD 400 M–1.9 B+ exposure on loss of a single large Containership.

* ★ Vessel operations are limited to a small number of deep-water ports, leading to an increased concentration of risks.

* ★ Average value per container varies between USD 35,000– USD 210,000.

World's Leading Containership Operators

Maersk (582)

MSC (495)

CMA CGM (430)

Evergreen (191)

PIL (164)

COSCO (162)

Hapag-Lloyd (154)

CSCL (136)

MOL (111)

NYK (109)

Hamburg-Sud (108)

APL (106)

Hanjin (98)

OOCL (92)

Yang Ming (89)

ZIM (83)

WAN HAI (81)

Containerships Age

0-5 Years ……………………………………..16

6-10 Years …………………………………...25

11-15 Years ………………………………….15

16-20 Years ………………………………… 14

>20 Years ………………………………….. 7

Unknown ………………………………….. 5

Containerships Location

Germany

North Atlantic (Bay of Biscay, English Channel, etc...)

Suez Canal

Indian Ocean (CMAL and South Afrika)

North Pacific (Japan)

Singapore

South China Sea (Vietnam)

Antwerp, Belgium

East China (Sea)

Gulf of Aden

Hong Kong

Netherlands

Safety & Shipping Review 2015

This is an annual review of trends and developments in shipping losses and safety.

* 75 large ships lost worldwide in 2014, down 32% year-on

* South China and South East Asian waters represent the top loss hotspots

* East Mediterranean and British Isles are associated with top location for incidents

* Cargo and fishing vessels account for over 50% of all losses

* Ship size growth raises risk management concerns: Industry should prepare for a loss ratio of I billion USD + loss

* The Industry needs to learn lessons from overreliance on e-navigation where Cyber Protection represents a major concern.

Sources: Allianz Global Corporate & Specialty

`Safety and Shipping Review´, London, 2015

The Marine Accident Investigation, Branch Southampton, UK, SO 15 2DZ, Report Number 9/2008, April 2008

Bibliography

Textbooks

Baughen (S), *Shipping Law,* London: Cavendish, 2004

Bennett (Howard), *The Law of Marine Insurance, 1996*

Berlingieri (F), *The Travaux Preparatoires of the Hague Rules and of the Hague-Visby Rules,* Antwerpen: CMI 1997

Briggs (A), *The Conflict of Laws,* Oxford: Oxford University Press, 2008

Carr (I), *International Trade Law,* London: Cavendish, 2005

Chua (Jason), *Law of International Trade,* Third Edition, Thomson, Sweet & Maxwell, 2005

Christou (Richard), *Sale and Supply of Goods and Services,* London, Sweet & Maxwell, 2007

De Wit, (Ralph), *Multimodal Transport: Carrier Liability and Documentation,* Lloyd's of London 1995; Supplement 2002

De Cruz (Peter), *Comparative Law In Changing World,* Third Edition, Routledge-Cavendish, London & New York, 2007, p.p: 1-27

Debatista (Charles), *Bills of lading in Export Trade* (Formerly, *The Sale of Goods Carried by Sea),* Third Edition Tp TOTTEL Publishing, 2009

Esin Orucu and Nelken (David), *Comparative Law: A Handbook,* Hart Publishing, Oxford and Portland, Oregon, 2007

Glass (David A.), *Freight Forwarding and Multimodal Transport Contract,* LLP, 2004

Goode (Roy), *Commercial Law,* Third Edition, Penguin Books, 2004

Harris (Brian), *Ridley's Law of the Carriage of Goods by Land, Sea and Air,* 8th Edition, Sweet & Maxwell, 2010

Hazelwood (Steven J.), *P&I Clubs: Law And Practice,* Third Edition, LLP, London, Hong Kong, 2000 (Mention should be made of the latest edition in 2010)

Hoeks (Marian), *Multimodal Transport Law: The law applicable to the multimodal contract for the carriage of goods,* 2010

Lamont-Black (S), Paul Bugden, *Goods in Transit (2nd edition),* Sweet & Maxwell, 2010

Lamont-Black (S), as formerly Simone Schnitzer, *Understanding International Trade Law,* LawMatters Publishing, 2006

Malcon A (Clarke), *International Carriage of Goodsd by Road: CMR,* 4th Edition, Lloyd's Transport Law Library, London 2003

Huybrechts (Marc A.), *Free on Board: Liber Amicorum Marc A. Huybrechts,* (784 pages), Intersentia, Co-editors Tetley (William), Stevens (F.) & Jacobsson (M), 2011

Merkin (Robert), *Insurance Disputes,* 2nd Edition, LLP, London, Hong Kong, 2003

Power (Vincent), *EU Shipping Law,* Third Edition, Informa, 2010

Rhidian (D), *The Modern Law of Marine Insurance,* Volume 3, Informa, London, 2009

Schramm (H.-J), *Freight Forwarder's Intermediary Role in Multimodal Transport Chains,* Contributions to Management Science, DOI 10.1007/978-3-7908-2775-0_6 Springer-Verlag Berlin, Heidelberg, 2012

Semak *(David), P&I Clubs and Practice,* 4th Edition, 2010

Tetley (William), *Marine Cargo Claims,* Fourth Edition, Volume 1, Carswell, les Editions Yvon Blais Inc.. 2008

Tetley (William), *Marine Cargo Claims,* Fourth Edition, Volume 2, Carswell, Les Editions Yvon Blais Inc… 2008

Thomas (D.R.), *New convention for the Carriage of Goods by Sea – the Rotterdam rules: an analysis of the UN convention on contract for the international carriage of goods wholly or partly by sea* (2009); Lawtext Publishing (Witney)

Trebilcock (Michael J.) and Howse (Robert), *The Regulation of International Trade,* Third Edition, Routledge, 2005

Urbina (Sebastian), *Legal Method and The Rule of Law,* Kluwer Law International, Martinus Nijhoff Publishers, 2002

Van Houte (Hans), *The Law of International Trade,* Second Edition, Sweet & Maxwell, A Thomson Company, London, Leuven, 2002

Wilson (John F.), *Carriage of Goods by sea,* 6th Edition, 6th Edition, Pearson, Longman

Journal Articles and Conference Papers

Ashton (R), 'A Comparison of the Legal Regulation of Carriage of Goods by Sea under Bills of Lading in Australia and Germany', In MLAANZ (1999): 24-63

Basedow (J), 'The Effects of Globalization on Private International Law', In Legal Aspects of Globalization, edited by Basedow (J) & Kono (T), Den Haag: Kluwer Law International, 2000, 1-10

Berlingieri (F), 'Door-to- Door Transport of Goods: Can Uniformity Be Achieved?', In Liber Amicorum Roger Roland, Brussels: Larcier, 2003, 37-55

Carr (I), 'The Current State of Multimodal Transport Law in the UK', In Multimodal Transport, edited by Kianku-Pampouki (A.), Brussels, Bruylant, 2000, 103-127

Chandler III (George F.), 'A comparison of "COGSA", the Hague/Hague-Visby Rules and the Hamburg Rules', HeinOnline- 15 J. Mar. L & Com. 233 1984

Clarke (M.A.), 'Harmonization of the Regulation of Carriage of Goods in Europe', TranspR (2002): 428-434

Crowley (ME), 'The Uniqueness of Admiralty and Maritime Law: The Limited Scope of the Cargo Liability Regime covering Carriage of Goods, Multimodal Transport' In Tul. L. Rev., 2005

Czerwenka (B), 'Scope of Application and Rules on Multimodal Transport Contracts', TranspR (2004): 297-303

Delebecque (P), 'The UNCITRAL Draft Instrument on the Carriage of Goods by Sea', CMI Yearbook 2003, 208-229

Eftestol-Wilhelmsson (Ellen), 'The Rotterdam Rules in a European Multimodal Context',(2010), 16 JML.

Eun Sup Lee, 'The Changing Liability System of Sea Carriers and Maritime Insurance: Focusing on the Enforcement of the Hamburg Rules', HeinOnline ... 15 Transnat'l Law, 241 2002, p.p: 241-255

Force (Robert), 'Multimodal Bill of Lading' In Admiralty and Maritime Law, Volume 2, C, 2008, Beard Books, Washington, D.C., USA

Frederick (David C.), 'Political Participation and Legal Reform in the International Maritime Rulemaking Process: From the Hague Rules to the Hamburg Rules', HeinOnline – 22 J. Mar. L. & Com. 81 1991

Gessner (Volkmar), 'Contractual Certainty in International Trade: Empirical and Theoretical Debates on Institutional Support for Global Economic Exchanges', ONATI International Series in Law and Society, Oxford & Portland, Oregon 2009

Herber (Rolf), 'The European Legal Experience with Multimodalism', Tulane Law Review, Vol. 64, Issues 2 & 3, p.p. 611-630, 64 TUL. L. Rev. 611 (1989-1990)

Hoeks (Marian) with Haak, K.F., 'Intermodal Transport under Unimodal Arrangements', Transportrecht 28 (3) 14, p.p.: 89-102

Hoeks (Marian) with Haak, K.F., 'Arrangements of International Transport in The Field of Conflicting Conventions", Journal of International Maritime Law, 2004 (11), p.p.: 422-434

Karan (Hakan), 'Any Need for a New International Instrument on the Carriage of Goods by Sea: The Rotterdam Rules?, In Journal of Maritime Law & Commerce, Vol. 42, No 3, July, 2011, p.p.: 441 – 451

Mukherjee (P. K.) & Abhinayan Basu Bal, 'A Legal and Economic Analysis of the Volume Contract Concept under the Rotterdam Rules: Selected Issues in Perspective' (24 pages), Paper presented in Rotterdam at the signature ceremony of the Rotterdam Rules, 2009

Pallares (Lorena Sales), 'A brief Approach to The Rotterdam Rules: Between Hope and Disappointment', In Journal of Maritime Law & Commerce, Vol. 42. No 3, July, 2011, p.p. 453-463

Reynolds (Francis), 'The Hague Rules, The Hague-Visby Rules and The Hamburg Rules' – 7 Austl. & N.Z. Mar. L.J. 16, 1990

Rhidian Thomas, 'And then there were the Rotterdam Rules', JIML, Nov. 5, 2008, p.p. 189-190

Rosaeg (E), 'The Applicability of Conventions for the Carriage of Goods and for Multimodal Transport', In Lloyd's maritime and commercial Law Quarterly, 2002, ISSN 0306-2945, Number 3, 2002, p.p. 316-335

Schoenbaum (Thomas J.), 'Multimodal Transport', In Admiralty and Maritime Law, Volume 2, 2004 (635 pages)

Shashikumar (N), Schatz (G.L.), 'The Impact of U.S. Regulatory Changes on International Movements', In Transportation Journal, Vol. 40, No 1 (Fall 2000), p.p.: 5-17, Penn State University Press

Tetley (William), 'A critique of/ and the Canadian response to the Rotterdam Rules' In Thomas (D.R.) Ed., New Convention for the carriage of goods by sea- the Rotterdam Rules: an analysis of the UN convention on contracts for the international carriage of goods wholly or partly by sea (2009; Lawtext Publishing: Witney)

Van Beelen (A), 'Netherlands Report on Multimodal Transport', Netherlands Reports to the fifteenth International Congress of Comparative Law, Bristol 1998, 333-345

Wood (Stephen G.), 'Multimodal Transportation: An American Perspective on Carrier Liability and Bill of Lading Issues', 46 Am. J. Comp. L. Supp. 403 1998, p.p: 403-420

International Conventions and other Legal Documents.

International Convention for the Unification of Certain Rules of Law relating to Bills of Lading (**"Hague Rules"**) and Protocol of Signature, Depository: Belgian Government, 1924

Protocol of 1968 to the International Convention for the Unification of Certain Rules of Law relating to the Bills of Lading, also called **"Hague Visby-Rules"**

Protocol of 1979 to the International Convention for the Unification of Certain Rules of Law relating to Bills of Lading

United Nations Convention on the Carriage of Goods by Sea referred to as **"Hamburg Rules"**, Hamburg, 1978, UN Secretariat

United Nations Convention on Contracts for the International Carriage of Goods Wholly or Partly by Sea, Rotterdam 2008, A/RES/63/122 (**"Rotterdam Rules"**)

Convention on The Contract for the International Carriage of Goods by Road (CMR) and Protocol of Signature, Geneva 19 May 1956, E/ECE 253 E/ECE TRANS 489

Uniform Rules Concerning the Contract for International Carriage of Goods by Rail (CIM),

(www.lexmercatoria on the 25th of June 2012)

Convention concerning International Carriage by Rail 1980 and Vilnius Protocol 1999 (at www. lexmercatoria on the 25th of June 2012)

Budapest Convention on the Contract for the Carriage of Goods by Inland Waterways CMNI/ CONF (99) 2/FINAL ECE/TRANS/CMNI/CONF/2/FINAL, the 3rd of October 2000 (Depository: the Government of Hungary), Budapest

Convention for the Unification of Certain Rules Relating to International Carriage by Air, Signed at Montreal on the 28th of May 1999 (Montreal Convention designed to replace The Warsaw Convention of 1929)

Council Decision 2001/539/EC 05 April 2001 on the Conclusion by the European Community of the Convention for the Unification of Certain rules for International Carriage by Air (The Montreal Convention), Official Journal L 194 of the 18th of July 2001

UNCTAD-ICC Rules for Multimodal Transport, UNCTAD SECRETARIAT SDTE/TLB/2? Add1, 9 October 2001

United Nations Convention on International Multimodal Transport of Goods (Geneva, 1980), UN (This convention did not enter into force).

Selected legislations

Belgian relevant legislation on Multimodal Transport

English Statutes on Multimodal Transport, including case law legislation

German Legislation on Multimodal Transport Rules

The Netherlands Legislation on Multimodal Transport

Summary of the Research Primary Legal Sources

The research legal sources are the following: Hague and Hague Visby Rules, Hamburg Rules and the recently adopted Rotterdam Rules, the British Carriage of Goods by Sea Act, the British shipping Act 1995, the National Legislations of Belgium, Germany and The Netherlands on Multimodal Carriage of Goods, the UNCTAD/ICC Rules on Multimodal Carriage of Goods, some Standard Forms of Contract on Multimodal Transport of Goods (BIMCO, GENCO, SITPRO and alike …), The British Insurance Act 1906, Insurance Policies and Practice in the Insurance Industry.

Eventually, the British Insurance Act 1906 has been recently modified by the "Insurance Act 2015 which introduces fundamental changes to Insurance Contract Law. It was passed as of the 12th of February 2015 and has now come into force. The aim of the Act is to ensure a better balance of interests between policy holders and insurers.

The reforms are likely to affect how parties underwrite risks, approach disclosure and due diligence, negotiate, discuss settlement, and litigate and so on.

Multimodal
Transport of Goods

{ In relation with the current Ship Owner's Liability Regimes as seen from a Claims Handling Perspective with regard to Protection & Indemnity Insurance
By Joseph Tshilomb Jonathan

Maj 2012 , Informatics Forum, EDINBURGH RESEARCH & INNOVATION, The University of Edinburgh , Edinburgh

*Unitization of goods culminating in the advent
of containerization leading to the subsequent
development of "Multimodal Transport"

*The present transportation pattern in international
trade is more towards total transportation companies
offering integrated air, sea, inland water, railways and
truck service

*Liability of the multimodal carrier or MTO and the
particular impact of these legal issues on the available
insurance cover in the transport sector

CARRIAGE OF GOODS

*Previous attempts to set a uniform, predictable
 and reliable legal regime applicable to the
international multimodal carrier have been
unsuccessful insofar.

*Resulting from different legal regimes concerned
with each mode of transport, the law of carriage of
goods has evolved historically and functionally
through separate transportation modes.

*As a result of the evaluation of the legal issues
mentioned above, the insurance industry has been
just coping with conflicting laws and regulations
while settling claims for damages or loss of goods or
for delays in delivery of goods.

Different Liability Limits, Forum
Shopping and Freedom of Contract...

The liability regime in multimodal carriage of goods seems unpredictable and unreliable.

METHODS OF THE RESEARCH:
*Legal Approach: method of solving conflicts in International Private Law (Conflict of laws and jurisdictions) and Comparative Law method
*Empirical Approach (Social sciences methods: survey related to the insurance industry and interviews with selected key actors)

Research Questions

*1 Given the different grounds of carrier liability and different limits of liability pertaining to the multimodal carriage of goods depending on various transportation modes in multimodal transport in the absence of a well harmonized liability regime, how will the insurance claim for damage, loss of goods or delay in cargo delivery be assessed?

*2 What is the impact of these legal issues in P&I and Cargo Insurance?

*3 Is there any need for harmonization of rules in the regime pertaining to the liability of the Multimodal Carrier (MTO) and the insurance covering the risks in multimodal carriage operations?

Research Legal Sources: Hague and Hague Visby Rules, Hamburg Rules and the recently adopted Rotterdam Rules, the British Carriage of goods by Sea Act, the British Shipping Act 1995, the National legislations of Germany and The Netherlands on Multimodal Carriage of Goods, The UNCTAD/ICC Rules on Multimodal Carriage of Goods, other Standard forms of contract on Multimodal Transport of Goods (BIMCO, GENCO, SITPRO and alike...), The British Insurance Act 1906 , Insurance policies and Practice in the Insurance Industry

THESIS STRUCTURE

At this stage of the research , the following structure is given:

Introduction

*Background to the thesis

*Theoretical perspectives

Chapter I Multimodal Transport of Goods: Legal Concept, History & Present Development

Chapter II The Multimodal Contract of Carriage of Goods

Chapter III The Rules of the Multimodal Contract and Unimodal Regimes

Chapter IV The Main Legal Issues in Multimodal Carriage of Goods and their Impact in Insurance (P&I Insurance and Cargo Insurance)

Chapter V Making a Claim for Damages in Multimodal Carriage

Chapter VI Insurance Claims Assessment

Chapter VII The Future Development in Insuring the risks in Multimodal Transport of Goods

Chapter VIII Harmonization of the Rules dealing with the Liability Regime in Multimodal Carriage of Goods and Improvement in Insurance Facilities

CONCLUSION

Importance of the thesis in the study of law

Contribution of the thesis in the topic area

Proposition on further studies in Multimodal Carriage of Goods and its impact s in the Insurance Industry

Thank you!

Presented by Joseph
Tshilomb
Panel Discussion led by
Professor Robin Williams
at the University of
Edinburgh
Edinburgh, May 2012

20ft GENERAL CARGO CONTAINER	Minimum Interior Dimensions			Door Dimensions		Cubic Capacity (Minimum)	Tare Weight (Maximum*)	Payload (Maximum)
	L	W	H	W	H			
20ft × 8ft × 8ft 6in	232in	91.7in	93.7in	91.7in	89.4in	1,154.8ft³	4,850lb	39,947lb
6.1m × 2.4m × 2.6m	5,900mm	2,330mm	2,380mm	2,330mm	2,270mm	32.7m³	220kg	18,120kg

*The tare weight for a 20ft general purpose container can vary between 3,747lb (1,700kg) and 4,850lb (2,200kg) depending on materials used in construction.

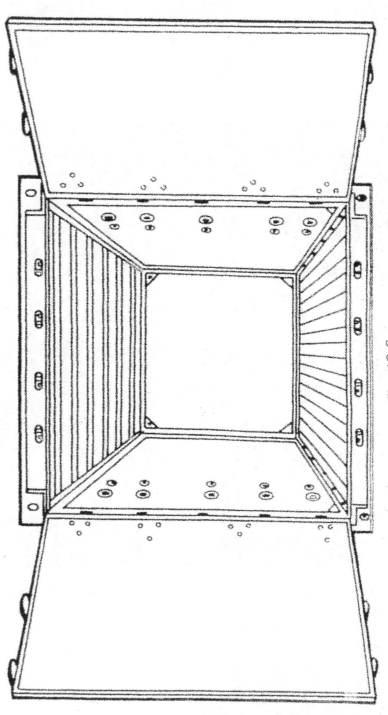

Fig. 12.3

20ft DRY BULK CONTAINERS

	Minimum Interior Dimensions			Door Dimensions		Cubic Capacity	Tare Weight	Payload
	L	W	H	W	H			
20ft × 8ft × 8ft	232in	91½in	86in	89½in	81½in	1,060ft³	6,150lb	38,650lb*
6.1m × 2.4m × 2.4m	5,893mm	2,324mm	2,184mm	2,267mm	2,064mm	30.01m³	2,789kg	17,531

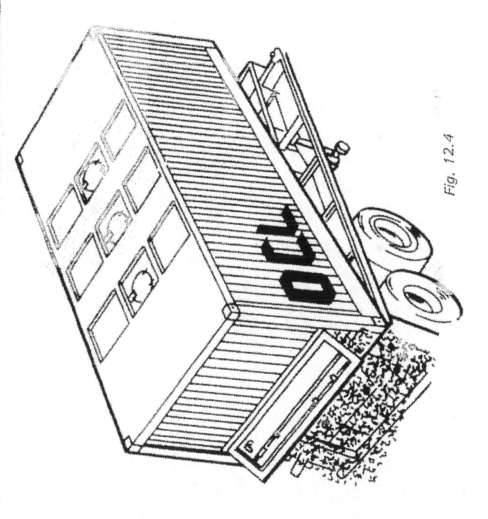

Fig. 12.4

Printed in the United States
By Bookmasters